what do we
know and
what should we
do about...?

abolishing
prisons

what do we
know and
what should we
do about...?

abolishing
prisons

Joe Sim

1 Oliver's Yard
55 City Road
London EC1Y 1SP

2455 Teller Road
Thousand Oaks
California 91320

Unit No 323–333, Third Floor, F-Block
International Trade Tower
Nehru Place, New Delhi – 110 019

8 Marina View Suite 43-053
Asia Square Tower 1
Singapore 018960

Editor: Rhoda Toweh
Editorial assistant: Pippa Wills
Production editor: Nicola Marshall
Copyeditor: Thea Watson
Proofreader: Anthony Green
Indexer: Silvia Benvenuto
Marketing manager: Fauzia Eastwood
Cover design: Bhairvi Vyas
Typeset by: C&M Digitals (P) Ltd, Chennai, India

Library of Congress Control Number: 2024947107

British Library Cataloguing in Publication data

A catalogue record for this book is available from the British Library

ISBN 978-1-5296-8461-2
ISBN 978-1-5296-8460-5 (pbk)

dedication

For Thomas Mathiesen and Mick Ryan. Pioneers for
a world without prisons.

titles in the series

contents

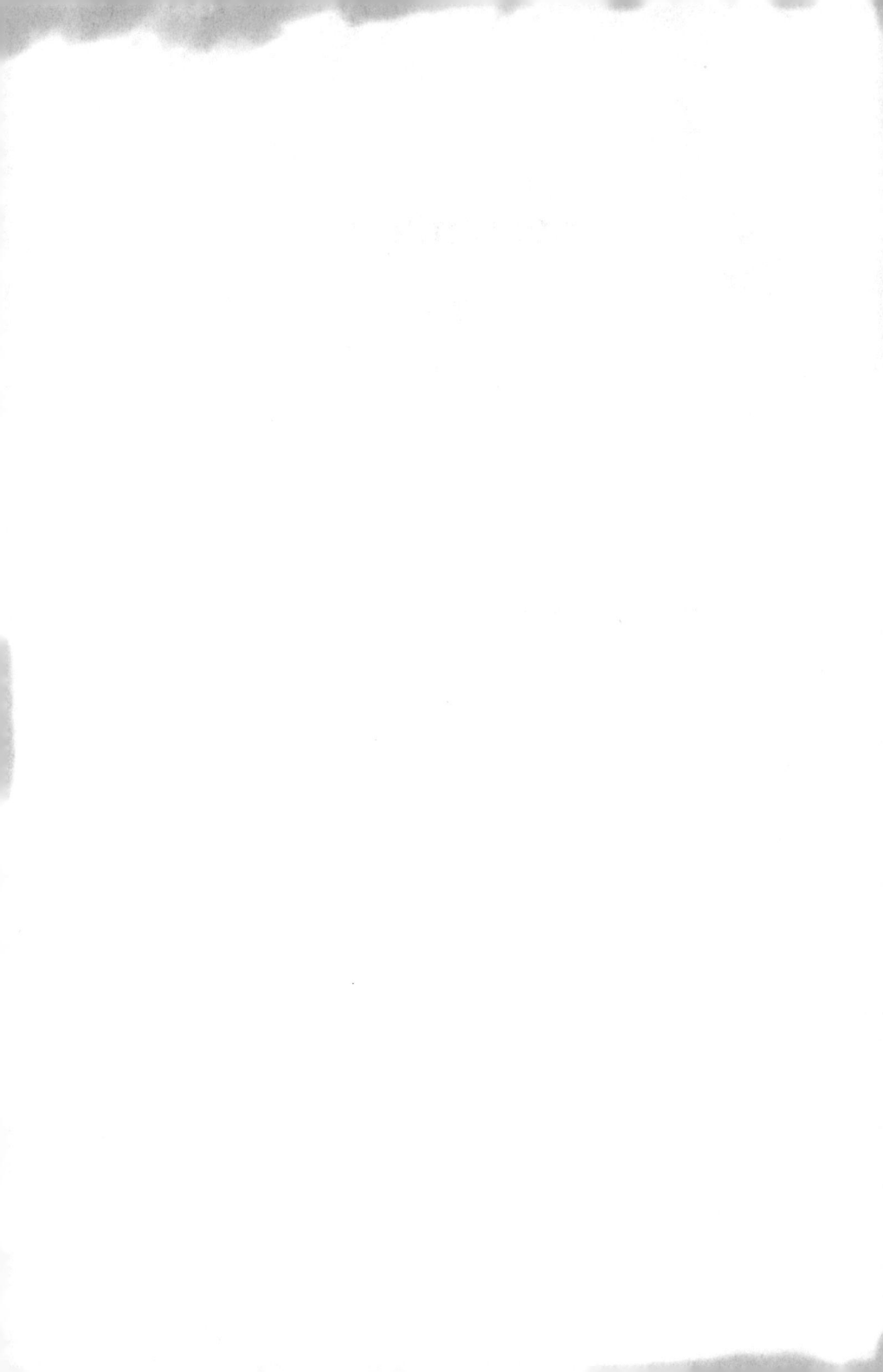

about the series

Every news bulletin carries stories which relate in some way to the social sciences – most obviously politics, economics and sociology, but also, often, anthropology, business studies, security studies, criminology, geography and many others.

Yet despite the existence of large numbers of academics who research these subjects, relatively little of their work is known to the general public.

There are many reasons for that, but, arguably, it is that the kinds of formats that social scientists publish in, and the way in which they write, are simply not accessible to the general public.

The guiding theme of this series is to provide a format and a way of writing which addresses this problem. Each book in the series is concerned with a topic of widespread public interest, and each is written in a way which is readily understandable to the general reader with no particular background knowledge.

The authors are academics with an established reputation and a track record of research in the relevant subject. They provide an overview of the research knowledge about the subject, whether this be long-established or reporting the most recent findings, widely accepted or still controversial. Often in public debate there is a demand for greater clarity about the facts, and that is one of the things the books in this series provide.

However, in social sciences, facts are often disputed and subject to different interpretations. They do not always, or even often, 'speak for themselves'. The authors therefore strive to show the different interpretations or the key controversies about their topics, but without getting bogged down in arcane academic arguments.

Not only can there be disputes about facts but also there are almost invariably different views on what should follow from these facts. And, in any case, public debate requires more of academics than just to report facts; it is also necessary to make suggestions and recommendations about the implications of these facts.

Thus each volume also contains ideas about 'what we should do' within each topic area. These are based upon the authors' knowledge of the field but also, inevitably, upon their own views, values and preferences. Readers may not agree with them, but the intention is to provoke thought and well-informed debate.

Chris Grey, Series Editor

Professor of Organization Studies

Royal Holloway, University of London

about the author

Joe Sim is Emeritus Professor of Criminology at Liverpool John Moores University, UK. He has written extensively about prisons, the state and punishment. He was a member of the Radical Alternatives to Prison Collective and is currently a trustee of the charity INQUEST.

acknowledgements

Thank you to Anette Ballinger for her support and encouragement; to David Scott whose 'abolitionist imagination' provided the original impetus for this book and which shines throughout the text; to Steve Tombs for discussing preventable and excess deaths and the data on health and safety at work; to Michael Ainsley, Nicola Marshall, Rhoda Ola-Said, Pippa Wills and Thea Watson at Sage for their exemplary input and guidance; and to the anonymous reviewers whose comments strengthened the original proposal.

introduction

In England and Wales, prisons are physical and psychological graveyards for the people inside. For centuries, ill-health, trauma, self-harm and preventable deaths have been central to their daily experiences. Between 1978 and March 2022, nearly 6900 people died in prison. Over 2700 of these deaths were self-inflicted (INQUEST and Ministry of Justice cited in Sim, 2023a: 900). And the deaths keep coming. In the year to September 2023, there were 304 deaths, 92 of which were self-inflicted, up 24% on the previous year. There were over 64,000 incidents of self-harm – 175 a day – a rise of 21% in a year. They had increased by 65% in women's prisons leading to an astonishing 6213 incidents per 1000 women inside (Ministry of Justice, 2023a). In Immigration Removal and Detention Centres, there were 42 deaths between 2000 and October 2024, 18 of which were self-inflicted (INQUEST, 2024a). In November 2023, there had 'been a self-harm incident or suicide attempt requiring medical treatment almost every day on average over the last nearly six years across the Home Office's largest immigration detention centres' (Taylor, 2023a).

These stark statistics graphically highlight the profound crisis in safety facing people in prison which gripped the institution in late 2023. The human costs of and the harms generated by the crisis were not restricted to prisons. Between April 2022 and March 2023, there were 1520 deaths – 4 a day – involving people under community supervision, an increase of 6% from the 1439 who had died the previous year (Ministry of Justice, 2023b). The sheer number of preventable deaths and incidents of self-harm challenged the widely disseminated myth that prisons, and community alternatives, were safe places which provided a duty of care to those who came into contact with them.

For people in prison, safety, or the lack of it, was not the only dimension to the crisis. It was multi-faceted, making the system virtually ungovernable. There was a record prison population – over 88,000, the highest in Western Europe – a lack of capacity, crowding, appalling living conditions, record numbers on remand, restless, confrontational staff and a systemic lack of purposeful activity leading to those inside spending endless, soul-crunching hours confined to their cells.

Responding to the crisis

What was the political response to what was the latest in a long history of crises? The dire situation led politicians and media commentators to describe prisons as 'broken'. However, this presupposed that they had *ever* been 'fixed', a highly dubious claim, as the evidence in this book demonstrates. As ever, in the race to the bottom of the law and order barrel, the then Conservative government, uncritically supported by the Labour opposition, reacted in a depressingly predictable manner. Patronising platitudes, extraordinary levels of hubris and desperate levels of political expediency dominated the collective mind-sets of both parties who were united around the self-serving narrative that building more prisons would defuse the crisis. They were intransigent in their opposition to *any* policy which appeared to undermine the totemic role of the prison in their highly politicised 'war on crime', or rather their 'war' on *some* crimes.

The response to those few politicians who have contested the law and order narrative – involving a corrosive network of other politicians, their aides and a hypocritical, populist press – has been brutal. This was exemplified by the treatment of Kenneth Clarke who was the Justice Secretary between 2010 and 2012 in the Conservative/Liberal coalition government. Clarke was hardly a prison abolitionist. Nonetheless, when he proposed to simplify the legal aid system, abolish short sentences and reduce the prison population, David Cameron, the then Prime Minister:

> [...] wanted him to increase mandatory sentences, and thus the prison population, and was encouraging him to sit with Rebekah Brooks, the editor of the *Sun,* and listen to her proposals to establish prison ships. *Twenty-five-year-old aides from Number 10 had lied about his health to get him excluded from television interviews* (Stewart, 2023: 69, emphasis added).

In October 2023, in an attempt to defuse the current crisis, the Justice Secretary announced a number of measures including: the largest prison building programme since Victorian times which would deliver 20,000 'modern rehabilitative prison places', deporting foreign national prisoners more quickly, refurbishing unused prison cells to increase capacity and spending £400 million 'for more prison places, enough for more than 800 new cells' (UK Parliament, 2023). According to the government's 2021 Spending Review, the new prison places would cost £3.8 billion, spread over three years (Sturge et al, 2023: 8). In pursuing this path, ministers were uncritically following the same, regressive precedent. For the last two centuries, the prison has 'always been offered as its own remedy...' to the recurring crises it has faced since its emergence at the end of the eighteenth century (Foucault, 1979: 268). Building more prisons is a political choice and is based on a series of interconnected myths and mis-representations concerning their highly debatable role in controlling crime or, more specifically, controlling the crimes of the poor *not* the crimes of the powerful. This is discussed more fully in Chapter 4.

This policy raises a key question. In terms of its official goals, what have prisons actually achieved in the last 200 years? Chapter 2 considers this question in the context of the reformist strategy which has been pursued during this period. In practice, reformism has resulted in an 'endless quest to perfect punishment or call it something different like rehabilitation and the result is always that we actually expand or replace or further entrench the punishment system' (Herskind, 2021). Those advocating, indeed sanctifying, reforming prisons have enjoyed an often-complicit relationship with the state. While appearing benevolent, progressive and stabilising reforms have been built on 'the irrational pursuit of harmful failures' (Carrier and Piche, 2015). Ultimately, they reinforce the 'stultifying idea that nothing lies beyond the prison' (Davis, 2003: 20).

Chapter 3 analyses the myths and misrepresentations about crime. It examines how a hypocritical 'truth' about criminality has been constructed and explores whose behaviour is criminalised by state institutions, and, as importantly, whose behaviour is not criminalised by these same institutions. The chapter also considers the myths and misrepresentations about people in prison, particularly the claim that the prison population is overwhelmingly made up of dangerous individuals. As the chapter indicates, the nature of the crimes for which people in prison are punished illustrates a very different reality to that propagated by the state, politicians and the mass media.

Chapter 4 addresses the myths and misrepresentations around prison regimes which justify the ongoing existence and continuous expansion of prisons while mystifying and hiding the grim reality and lived experiences of the people inside. At the same time, they reinforce the false, misguided claim that prisons are essential if crime is to be controlled and social order maintained.

Against reformism, for abolition

Having explored the myths and misrepresentations around reformism, crime and prisons in the previous chapters, Chapter 5 outlines the case for abolishing prisons in England and Wales. The state and the academic and liberal prison reform industry continuously seek to bend the narrative about prisons towards reforms which 'work' thereby supporting policies considered 'realistic' in order to 'modernise' the institution. It is an approach which is based on 'what already exists' (Unger, cited in Williams, 2013) and not on what *could be*.

Abolitionists have challenged this position. For them, the prison is a 'fiasco' (Mathiesen, 2000: 141). If it is *the* answer to crime and social harm, then the wrong questions are being asked. The institution is a malignant force and a moral disgrace. Abolitionists are committed to shining a critical spotlight on the myths around prisons and to the often-hideous reality of life inside, the often-deadly harms prisons generate, the abject failure to fulfil their official goals and their centuries-old, policy failures. They are not sites for rehabilitation but are blistering places of 'punishment for misery' which desecrate the human spirit (Marx, cited in Sim, 2019). People in prison are punished and degraded and lead spectral, bereft lives in a corrosive environment, where systemic indifference towards them as human beings prevails. The searing, punitive relentlessness of institutional regimes physically shred and psychologically traumatise many of them as the number of deaths and incidents of self-harm indicate. Although written in a different context, Dorian Lynskey's words apply to their physical and psychological state; they are 'derelict husks' who do not live but 'haunt the world' (Lynskey, 2024: 62 and 70).

In confronting the existence of prisons, abolitionists have been caricatured as out-of-touch idealists. For non-abolitionists, a world without prisons is unimaginable. To paraphrase Mark Fisher (2009: 1), the institution has become so normalised in political and popular consciousness that, 'it's easier to imagine the end of the world than the end of the prison'. For abolitionists, however, it *is* possible to imagine a world without prisons. Chapter 5 also challenges the misinformed claim that abolitionists do not have 'realistic' policies for changing prisons. On the contrary, they advocate a range of 'abolitionist alternatives' (Davis, 2003: 109). If implemented, they would defuse the prison crisis, radically transform the current dire situation, drastically reduce victimisation, support victims and survivors and deliver social justice for all.

Central to abolitionism is the moral and political commitment to ensuring the safety, security and protection of people in prison, and in the wider society, not only from legally defined crimes but also from the systemic, devastating social harms generated by the law-breaking activities of those who exercise economic, political and patriarchal power – corporate executives, state agents and violent men. These harms are often more destructive and damaging for human beings than the acts and actions criminalised by the law from which prisons offer little or no protection.

To be clear, this is *not* an argument for ignoring legally defined crimes or dismissing their often-traumatic impact on victims, survivors and their families. However, it *is* an argument for bringing social harms out of the shadows, recognising the human misery they cause and removing the insidious, hypocritical culture of immunity and impunity which shields and protects those who engage in such destructive behaviour. This culture allows the powerful to deny their culpability for the outcomes of their actions and non-actions, including the thousands of preventable deaths they generate each year which are still too often mystified, dismissed and ignored.

Having established the issues with which this book is concerned, Chapter 2 outlines a brief history of prison reform over the last two hundred years and traces the shifting, often-contradictory goals of penal policy. It also outlines an alternative history which illustrates the prison's historical role in punishing, disciplining and controlling those living, or simply existing, on the margins of a deeply unequal society built on lacerating social divisions which have scarred, skewered and destroyed lives, families and communities over this period.

background: a history of failure and success

This chapter briefly addresses four issues. First, it considers the discourse of progressive, liberal reform which has dominated the historical narrative about prisons and other state institutions. Second, it explores an alternative, critical history of prisons which argues prisons have *not* failed. Rather, they have been successful in disciplining and punishing those often-vulnerable people existing on the margins of a compassionless, divided society. Third, it documents the official, overlapping goals of the prison which have justified the institution's existence and expansion for two hundred years. Finally, it provides an alternative, critical analysis of these goals, which, even on their own terms, have failed, often catastrophically, during this period.

Two centuries of progress?

Prisons became the dominant method of state punishment at the end of the eighteenth century. Previously, using the stocks, transportation to the 'colonies' and destroying the body through torture and capital punishment were the state's preferred responses to crime. For liberals, the emergence of prisons was a progressive, modernising policy which represented a shift in punishment where the brutality of the pre-modern age was replaced by a modern, humanitarian, enlightened approach to crime and deviance.

However, from the beginning, prisons were in a state of 'permacrisis' (Murji, 2023: 21). It is a concept which has been applied to the police but which also can be applied to prisons. In criticisms which resonate today, they were denounced for failing to fulfil their official goals, diminish the crime rate and reduce reoffending. They also produced delinquency, encouraged loyalty between prisoners, stigmatised those inside which continued after they were released and condemned prisoners' families to a life of destitution (Foucault, 1979: 264–268). Despite these criticisms, the state's response has not faltered over the decades:

> Word for word, from one century to the other, the same fundamental propositions are repeated. They reappear in each new, hard-won, finally accepted formulation of a reform that has hitherto been lacking. The same sentences, or almost the same could have been borrowed from other 'fruitful' periods of reform […] So successful has the prison been that, after a century and a half of 'failures' the prison still exists, producing the same results and there is the greatest reluctance to dispense with it (Foucault, 1979: 268 and 270).

The state's cure for making prisons 'better' has been built on instigating piecemeal reform to defuse the immediate crisis until the next one occurs. Again, as with the police, the cure has been depressingly predictable. The state has pursued:

> […] repackaged versions of the same old remedies […] here is a forgetting of the extent to which such remedies have been tried already: there is no assessment of what did and did not work in the past, and no-one confronts the basic question of why anything should be different this time […] Apart from the circularity of the repertoire of actions proposed after every crisis, there is only one certainty in this zombie landscape: the next [prison] crisis is a matter of when not if (Murji, 2023: 23, 29 and 31).

Contemporary prisons have experienced a cascade of futile, expedient reforms which have done little, if anything, to deal with the underlying structural issues driving crisis after crisis. They have included: resetting industrial relations; offering better pay; developing an enhanced role for staff through Fresh Start; pursuing the Decency Agenda; introducing better management structures; building more prisons with a different architectural design; instituting inquiries into previous crises such as the May Report in 1979 and the Woolf Report in 1991; imposing audits and Key Performance Indicators; replacing prison governors; changing staff in prison service headquarters; instituting changes specifically aimed at women prisoners; and paying lip service to prisoners' rights. While the list of reforms is long, their inpact has been negligible. And some reforms have made the situation worse. The men involved in the Sex Offender Treatment Programme (STOP), introduced in 2012, became *more* harmful in terms of their propensity for sexual violence. Despite this, the Ministry of Justice unlawfully continued to operate the programme until 2017 (Shaw, 2019).

An alternative history

There is an alternative history which challenges the dominant narrative of progressive, liberal reformism, which assumes that:

> [...] the violence, systemic bias, and institutional dysfunction of carceral systems are deviations and errors [...] rather than the fundamental and systemic features of those systems. [...] This enables reforms that legitimate, reinforce, and augment the carceral state and ultimately serve to reproduce its mechanisms of violence and oppression (Rodriguez, cited in Bell, 2021).

This alternative history focuses on the prison's function *not* in terms of the success or failure of its official goals but rather its role in the exercise of state power which reinforces the social order of a compassionless, structurally unequal society. Given that there have been 200 years of endless reforms, then:

> [...] the most salutary lesson of revisionist history is that the contemporary prison system is *the reformed prison system*. The crisis in the prisons is the crisis of reform, the seeds of which were sown when the prisons were reconstituted in the early nineteenth century as part of a wider struggle to impose a new form of class domination (Fitzgerald and Sim, 1982: 165, original emphasis).

Furthermore, prisons, and the other state institutions such as workhouses and the new police which also emerged 200 years ago, did *not* operate neutrally, objectively and universally. Rather, they were integral to a newly emerging state machine which ruthlessly targeted, criminalised, detained and punished specific groups: the poor, the unemployed, the morally 'compromised' and the deviant. The daily regimes in these 'complete and austere institutions' were drenched in discipline, correction, punishment, moral cleansing, isolation, observation and surveillance (Foucault, 1979: 231–256). The goal was the normalisation of the deviant. People in institutions were to be trained to be good, docile workers, or in the case of 'deviant' women – those labelled as criminals, spinsters, sexually 'deviant' and insane – normalisation meant making them respectable, virtuous homemakers through being subjected to often-brutal punishment, including sexual violence asylums (Ussher, 1991).

There are different strands within this alternative history, which are beyond the scope of this book to explore (Garland, 1990). However, what unites them is a critical understanding of prison history and state institutions, more generally. This history conceptualises their role as being *less* concerned with crime control, whatever their official goals claimed, and *more* concerned with maintaining a deeply divided social order based on structural inequalities and social divisions. So while the prison might have failed to fulfil its official goals, for Michel Foucault, it has been politically and ideologically successful:

[...] which is why it has never been abandoned [...] the prison does not control the criminal so much as control the working class by creating the criminal, and, for Foucault, this is the unspoken rationale for its persistence [...] The prison is thus retained for its failures and not in spite of them (Garland, 1990: 149–150).

Like its historical predecessor, the contemporary prison is *not* a failure. The institution performs a number of distinct roles, as noted above, including: detaining, controlling and punishing those often-vulnerable people enduring life on the margins of a grossly unequal society, who are then 'conveniently forgotten'; diverting attention from acts which are 'socially dangerous [...] increasingly being committed by individuals and classes with power in society'; symbolically constructing and stigmatising people in prison as the *only* law breakers in the wider society despite the widespread and endemic nature of law-breaking; and generating legitimacy for ill-informed politicians who *appear* to be taking action against crime:

By relying on the prison, by building prisons, by building more prisons, by passing legislation containing longer prison sentences, the actors on the political level of our own times thus obtain a method of showing that they act on crime as a category of behaviour, that they do something about it, that something is presumably being done about law and order [...] (Mathiesen, 2000: 143).

This raises another question: who have been the targets of punishment over the last two centuries? The praxis of punishment is not neutral nor does it exist in a social or political vacuum: '[...]by nature of the particular groups it serves to control; the power relations in society impact significantly on the make-up of prison populations [...]' (Behan and Stark, 2023: 46). In other words, the prison system was, and is, not broken as many commentators have claimed. Rather, it was and is '[...] functioning as intended – as a form of surveillance, control and punishment and as a way to conceal rather than address society's problems' (Law: 2021: 150).

The prison's official goals

The state's addiction to the reformist/modernisation discourse is inextricably tied to the attempt to ensure prisons fulfil their official goals including moral reform, individual and collective deterrence, crime prevention, incapacitation, punishment, retribution and rehabilitation (Mathiesen, 2000). These overlapping, intertwining goals have justified the prison's existence over the last 200 years. In theory, they were, and are, designed to produce the golden fleece of penology, namely, the perfect prison which will cut crime, reduce reoffending and change people for the better.

Again, however, there is an alternative, critical perspective which challenges the official narrative. Like the reforms discussed above, the goals of the prison are constantly repackaged through a 'penal-merry-go-round' which deflects attention from the reality of long-term failure (Scott, 2018: 136). And whatever their official goals, prisons have *always* operated as places of punishment and pain. People in prison do not experience their regimes as providing a 'service', as in the 'prison service'. This is a myth. Rather, they experience it as a force. They have been consistently constructed as *less eligible subjects*, meaning that their experience inside must always be worse than the experiences of the law-abiding majority (or those who claim to be the law-abiding majority) outside the prison walls. Crime, at least for the poor, must not pay and must *not* be seen to pay. Contemporary prisons have largely failed to escape from the iron grip of less eligibility established in the nineteenth century. Hence, in popular and political consciousness, prisons must not operate as 'holiday camps', an issue which is discussed in Chapter 4. This mentality underpins the general lack of moral concern, both inside and outside, about the lived experiences of people in prison. As less eligible subjects, they are stigmatised as a distinct immoral and amoral class who are undeserving of compassion, sympathy and empathy. In short, 'the indignities, deaths and injuries' people in prison suffer 'are not considered as significant as those befalling people on the outside because the socially dead prisoner is no longer eligible for our care and concern' (Scott, 2020a: 106). Less eligibility also undermines the idea that being locked up – the deprivation of liberty – should be punishment enough and that the individual should not suffer further punishment in prison.

At different historical moments, less eligibility has been particularly pronounced. In the mid-to-late nineteenth century, a brutal, repressive philosophy, based on individual and collective deterrence, operated. Prisoners' testimonies and autobiographies damned prison regimes for their physical and psychological brutality and the deaths that resulted from this brutality (Sim, 1990). From the late nineteenth century, and for most of the twentieth century, the state's legitimating mantra justifying the prison's existence was rehabilitation. This mantra – that people in prison could be treated and trained to lead a 'good and useful life' – still prevails despite the compelling evidence that prisons do not rehabilitate those inside. In fact, as Chapter 4 illustrates, despite the odd exception, rehabilitation has never been put into practice in prisons. It was more myth than reality. Over the last two centuries, prisoners' autobiographies, critical academics and the prisoners' rights movement have described a very different, brutal reality to that espoused by the state's defence of rehabilitation (Scott, 2020b). The number of protests since 1969, often against the brutality of prison regimes including the 25-day disturbance at Strangeways in 1990, indicates that the material and psychological conditions inside prisons have changed very little despite the state's claim that the rehabilitation of people inside is the central goal of prison regimes.

For critics, behind the discourse of rehabilitation lay the grim reality experienced by people in prison who were treated as less than human with often devastating consequences. They were subjugated in bleak, retributive, unforgiving regimes, where systemic indifference, debasement, terror, trauma, punitive degradation and lacerating callousness rather than rehabilitative care and compassion, prevailed. People in prison still experience contemporary regimes as dreaded sites of psychological disintegration which impact differentially on minority ethnic prisoners, women and girls, younger and older prisoners, LGBTQ+ prisoners and prisoners with disabilities.

Prisons deform people rather than reform them: '[n]ot only can we most certainly say that the prison does not rehabilitate... in fact it *de*habilitates'

(Mathiesen, 2000: 53, original emphasis). Within contemporary prisons, even if it was part of penal policy which is highly debatable, 'rehabilitation has largely refocussed on risk management and control rather than supporting individuals to change' (Garland, cited in Bhui, 2024: 31). Furthermore, rehabilitation will not work in a deeply divided, structurally unequal society:

> [...] re-integration, re-settlement or re-entry are often used instead of re-habilitation. Yet all of these terms, with their English prefix 're', imply that the law breakers or ex-prisoners, who are to be 're-habilitated'/'re-integrated'/'re-settled' or 're-stored', previously occupied a social state or status to which it is desirable they should be returned. Not so. The majority of prisoners worldwide have, prior to their imprisonment, usually been so economically and/or socially disadvantaged that they have nothing to which they can be advantageously rehabilitated (Carlen, 2012).

Uncritically sanctifying rehabilitation as the prison's central goal reinforces the state's dubious claim that rehabilitating prisoners *did* operate in practice at different historical periods such as in the immediate post-war period and the 1950s, a period widely regarded as consensual and moderate compared with the convulsive, confrontational politics which have occurred since then. However, this account ignores a key question: what was the reality like on the ground in state institutions and in the wider society for different social groups? In many ways, this was *not* a period of consensus and harmony that is often claimed.

Prisoners' accounts again described a different reality including institutionalised violence in punishment blocks and 'kickings by groups of warders' (Probyn, cited in Sim, 1990: 88). Women who were labelled as 'depressed' described being subjected to electro-convulsive 'therapies' and pre-frontal lobotomies in asylums (Showalter, 1987). Newly arrived immigrants suffered racist attacks and daily harassment not only by the public, but also by the police (Gilroy, 2013). And there were the miscarriages of justice, the lack of concern about domestic and homophobic violence and abroad there was the brutal enforcement of imperialist policies manifested in judicially endorsed executions against those living under colonial rule (Elkins, 2022). This was hardly a period of rehabilitation and compassion either in prisons, other state institutions or in the wider society.

Two other goals have justified the prison's existence: deterrence and incapacitation. These goals have also been criticised. The sheer extent of crime and social harm raises serious questions about the impact of the prison as a deterrent both to individuals and to the wider collective. The claim that prisons will deter individuals and thereby generate a fall in the crime rate is highly contentious. This point was made by the House of Commons Justice Committee over ten years ago when it noted that it was 'virtually impossible to find a causal link between the use of prison and a fall in crime rates' (cited in Bhui, 2024: 72).

Incapacitating dangerous individuals is one of the central issues facing prisons and the wider society. And while this issue might appear to be straight-forward, in fact there are a number of important questions which the state, politicians and the media rarely, if ever, ask. How is dangerousness defined? Can dangerousness be predicted? What impact does imprisonment have in ensuring the safety, security and protection of different groups such as women and girls? This issue is addressed in Chapter 4.

Conclusion

In 1978, the historian Michael Ignatieff challenged the idea of the historical inevitability of progress. Given the ongoing centrality of the discourse of reformism and the lack of a critical, historical understanding, indeed collective amnesia amongst politicians, media commentators and state agents, Ignatieff's words provide a chilling, highly relevant warning about forgetting the past:

[History] can help to pierce through the rhetoric that ceaselessly presents the further consolidation of carceral power as a 'reform'.

As much as anything else, it is this suffocating vision of the past that legitimates the abuses of the present and seeks to adjust us to the cruelties of the future (Ignatieff, 1978: 220).

For those who support this critical perspective, the role of the prison has changed little over the last 200 years. The institution has been integral to a system which has targeted, criminalised and punished those at the bottom of the ferocious ladder of social inequality. In other words, people in prison have *never* been drawn evenly from the wider population *nor* do the crimes for which they have been imprisoned indicate the full extent of the law-breaking behaviour prevalent throughout the wider society. Rather, it is a select few lawbreakers – people who have been discarded, dehumanised and disposed of – who have been, and continue to be, detained, disciplined and punished in state institutions.

The next chapter considers this issue through dissecting what is known, *and* not known, both about crime and the contemporary prison population.

what do we know, and not know, about crime and the prison population?

This chapter explores the hypocritical myths and misrepresentations surrounding the nature and extent of crime. It then considers the state and media-defined 'truth' about people in prison and the crimes for which they have been sentenced. This discussion reveals that not only is criminal behaviour widespread but that far from containing overwhelmingly dangerous individuals, prisons are essentially social dustbins, regulating and punishing often-vulnerable people existing on the margins of a deeply unequal, compassionless society.

The 'truth' about crime

This is not a chapter about criminal statistics. However, before analysing the myths and misrepresentations surrounding people in prison, it addresses three points concerning official criminal statistics which play a key role in the social construction of the state's 'truth' about crime.

First, there is the political and popular hypocrisy surrounding crime. The sheer extent of socialy harmful behaviour, whether defined by the criminal law or not, is denied by the state, politicians, the media and the general population. In reality, crime is endemic across the social landscape, whatever the individual's background. In other words, '... conventional crime studies have generally neglected to address growing evidence that *most people habitually violate the law*' (Woodall, 2018: 117, emphasis added). Thus, the relentless focus on the small number of people in prison who are labelled as the *only* 'real' criminals who deserve punishment is simply wrong.

Second, official criminal statistics are immensely problematic in reflecting the nature and extent of crime. It is not only prison abolitionists who have made this point. In 1982, Lord Lane, the then Lord Chief Justice, hardly a bastion of radicalism given his role in a number of disputed convictions and miscarriages of justice, told the House of Lords that, '[y]our Lordships' attention has been directed properly to the courts, to the police and to statistics. So far as statistics are concerned, I propose to say nothing except that they are mostly misleading and very largely unintelligible'. For good measure, he added that it had 'become apparent, as the noble Lord, Lord Wigoder, has already said, prison never did anyone any good' (Hansard, 1982: column 987). Forty years on from Lord Lane's still relevant points, politicians, in particular, continue to use criminal statistics as a socially poisonous means to justify their often-retributive law and order ends and secure their political and moral authority. If they can claim crime has fallen due to their policies then by their cynical logic the votes will follow. And the bigger the percentage fall, the better for making headlines, no matter how misconceived, erroneous and misinformed that claim might be.

In November 2023, while still Prime Minister, Rishi Sunak claimed he was '[...] pleased to see that under this Government, by the most recent year for which we have data, crime had decreased by 56% since 2010' (Hansard, 2023: column 646). Coincidently, or not, this was the year that Sunak's Conservative party came to power. His assertion was based on figures from the Crime Survey for England and Wales (CSEW). Despite the survey's limitations, including its restricted definition of violence which results in the underestimation of male violence against women and girls (Davies et al, 2024), the Office for National Statistics (ONS) claims that it provides a clearer picture of crime than the official criminal statistics which are based on the vicissitudes of public reporting and police recording practices.

However, according to the ONS, the fall of 56% to which Sunak referred '[...] represents all CSEW crime *excluding* fraud and computer misuse, this is because fraud and computer misuse was not captured in the survey at this time' (personal communication, ONS, 20 November 2023, emphasis added). Sunak did not refer to the exclusion of these categories. Why? If fraud and computer misuse *had* been included, the number of crimes recorded between July 2022 and June 2023 indicated a rise from 4,185,000 to 8,420,000. And even more problematically, while fraud was happening on a widespread scale, as ever, there was:

> [...] a near absence of policing. Less than 1 per cent of reports lead to prosecution and the Commons public accounts committee recently reported [2023], of the 20,000 police recruits just 2 per cent [400] will specialise in fraud – even though it accounts for 40 per cent of all crime (*Private Eye*, 2023: 8).

Third, even if crime *was* rising, it does not follow that building more prisons provides the solution. According to the National Audit Office, '[...] there is no link between the prison population and levels of crime' (cited in Prison Reform Trust, 2024: 14). This point also applied to international jurisdictions.

However, there *is* a clearer link between criminalisation, the imprisonment rate and structural inequality. In a system based on institutionalised criminal *injustice*, those who are systematically targeted by the state – overwhelmingly, powerless and often-vulnerable individuals – who are often coercively and degradingly processed through its institutions, stand in direct contrast to the non-targeting of, and non-response to, those in positions of power whose behaviour generates widespread, devastating social harms. In short:

[…] the distribution of punishment between the poor and the rich is driven by political choice. In part this is reflected in how penal codes are designed, punishing street crime more harshly than white-collar crime and partly this is due to the street-level politics of law enforcement […] large-scale punishment projects depend significantly on the dehumanisation of the poor and the powerless. Harsh punishment requires a profound suspension of human compassion (Western, 2018: 134–135).

'Churning' human beings

Before discussing who is in prison, and the crimes for which they have been prosecuted and sentenced, there are two important points to consider. First, people in prison constitute a small number of 'the far larger universe of people whose lives are affected by the criminal justice system' (Sawyer and Wagner, 2020). The yearly 'churning' of human beings (Sawyer and Wagner, 2020) – overwhelmingly poor, destitute and increasingly racialised – through the courts, prisons, other state and private institutions and the parole and probation systems, is rarely discussed by politicians and the media. If they did consider this data, they would see that in the year ending June 2023, 1.42 million people 'were dealt with' by the criminal justice system (Ministry of Justice, 2024a), over 44,000 people were sentenced to prison (Prison Reform Trust, 2024: 14) while over 238,000 people were on probation (Ministry of Justice, 2024b: 15). There were also thousands of people detained in other state and private institutions: young offender institutions; secure training centres; secure children's homes; military prisons; and psychiatric hospitals. In March 2020, 23,000 asylum seekers were held at different derention sites (Burnett, 2022: 41).

Second, the sheer number of people who experience 'churning' is mystified and hidden, as is the nature of their offences. This is due to the political and media focus on the Average Daily Population (ADP). This refers to people in prison who are serving sentences on a particular day and suggests that the prison population is made up of dangerous indi-viduals. At the end of March 2024, those in custody for violence against the person 'accounted for the highest proportion of prisoners (32%). Sexual offences was the second highest category for adults (20%) while for juveniles this was robbery (14%)' (Sturge, 2024: 12). When the number of life and indeterminate sentenced prisoners is considered, again prisons appear to be filled with dangerous individuals. In 2022, there were just under 6700 life sentence prisoners alone held in English and Welsh pris-ons (Council of Europe, cited in Prison Reform Trust, 2024: 20).

However, when the focus switches from the ADP to *who* is actually prosecuted and sentenced during the course of a year, and for *what* crimes, then a very different picture emerges.

Prosecuting the poor

Churning begins at the prosecution stage where the poor, the physically and mentally vulnerable, the disabled and the elderly are processed, often quickly and ignominiously, through the system. The Single Justice Procedure (SJP), established in 2015, illustrates this point. This 'proce-dure' was designed to fast-track the accused and to cut court costs. In practice, hearings lacked transparency and were held behind closed doors with few legal safeguards for those being processed. Magistrates dealt with around 40,000 cases a month with cases taking between 30 and 40 seconds while evidence was ignored (BBC, 2024). People charged have included:

> [...] an 84-year-old pensioner prosecuted by the DVLA [Driving and Vehicle Licensing Agency] and fined £1876 for not paying £93 in road tax and a 78-year-old woman with schizophrenia and dementia who was convicted of not having vehicle insurance. Her daughter had written to say the offence happened when she had fallen ill and was admitted to hospital, but she was issued with the £156 fine nonetheless (Meadows, 2023).

There are other examples. Between 2010 and 2019, there were 15,000 prosecutions for begging, resulting in 12,493 convictions (Cromarty et al, cited in Sim, 2023a: 887). And between 2019 and early 2024, nearly 2500 homeless people were arrested under the 1824 Vagrancy Act (Walker, 2024). In other areas, one person who, in 2024, gained 30p a week while claiming a carer's allowance for his son who had learning difficulties, and who was addicted to heroin, was 'dragged through the courts and had to sell his home to pay back almost £20,000 in benefit overpayments'. He was 'fighting to clear his name after the Department for Work and Pensions (DWP) acknowledged he made an innocent mistake' (Pidd, 2024). When they have been forced to face the courts, carers have not been legally represented (Halliday, 2024).

In 2017, '30% of all criminal prosecutions of any kind, against women were for non-payment of the TV licence' (Sakande, 2021). By February 2024, almost 1000 people a week, 70% of them women, were being prosecuted for this offence. These cases included a hospital patient and a woman who had forgotten to pay because she had a brain injury (Williams, 2024).

Rona Epstein researched the cases of 108 men and 37 women who were charged with contempt of court between 2019 and 2022. Their powerful and often-poignant testimonies illustrate the link between the criminalisation of poverty and the punishment of the poor. Their stories are reproduced in detail below because they are rarely heard through the law and order thunder that has become normalised. They capture one of the central themes of this book. Often-vulnerable people are being churned through, and punished by, a system devoid of empathy, compassion and humanity:

Many of these [cases] concerned people who appeared to be particularly vulnerable. Eighty-one immediate imprisonments were ordered and 64 suspended, and three fines imposed ranging from £120 to £250. The reports do not indicate whether or how a means enquiry was made before these fines were imposed. The largest group of 44 cases concerned nuisance to neighbours including noise, bad language, threats, and shouting. Thirty-two cases involved individuals found to be in prohibited areas. There were twelve cases related to drug dealing or possession, six of begging and sleeping rough. For example, in August 2019 Birmingham County Court sentenced James M. to 26 weeks immediate imprisonment for breaching an injunction by begging... The same punishment was imposed on Martin G. for sleeping rough and possession of a crack pipe. Reading the reports we find an array of mental health issues. Sentencing Evelyn C. to four weeks' suspended imprisonment, the court said 'there are underlying mental health issues' and that there has been involvement with mental health professionals. She is 76 years old, being threatened with eviction; her offence was making a noise outside her flat, banging doors, shouting and swearing. On 22 February 2021 – in full lockdown because of the Covid-19 pandemic – Clerkenwell and Shoreditch County Court committed Mr Tack to six weeks' immediate imprisonment, for breaking an injunction not to make a noise in the early hours...

In addition, the court may make an order of a fine or costs. Michael R., a man who was homeless and an alcoholic was found to be in a prohibited place (his father's home) and was ordered to pay costs of £2093 [...] Brentford County Court imposed a fine of £120 on two contemnors [people who are found to be in contempt of court] [...] Nicholas M. fed pigeons on his balcony, which caused mess from birds: he was committed to 15 weeks' immediate custody on 12.6. 20... Joyce N. was committed to 8 weeks' immediate imprisonment on 19 June 2020 by Manchester County Court, for breaking an injunction not to be in a prohibited place... And... on 21.2.21 Mr Batty was sent to prison for one year for two incidents of begging (Epstein, 2022).

People in prison

As noted above, in the year to June 2023, over 44,000 people were sentenced to prison. Within this figure, 58% had committed a non-violent offence while 37% were sentenced to six months or less (Prison Reform Trust, 2024: 14). In the case of women, 69% of those sentenced had 'committed a non-violent offence'. In 2022, there were more women sent to prison for theft 'than for criminal damage and arson, drug offences, possession of weapons, robbery, and sexual offences combined' (Prison Reform Trust, 2024: 49). Despite the recognised negative impact and ineffectiveness of short sentences, over half were sentenced to less than six months (Prison Reform Trust, 2023a).

Therefore, who is in prison and for what crimes, further undermines the dominant 'truth' about dangerous prisoners. For centuries, people inside have been consistently drawn from the poorest and most deprived sections of the wider population (Garland, 1985). In 1967, a study of women prisoners found that 'like most males in prison' they 'tended to come from the manual and unskilled social class groups, many had young children already in the care of the local authority and a significant minority had serious marital problems' (cited in Mott, 1985: 48). Five years later, another study found that one third of the 811 men involved were homeless, 10% were both homeless and suffering from mental ill-health and 75% were manual workers (Mott, 1985: 19). In 1991, the Prison Reform Trust published *The Identikit Prisoner.* The report showed that the pre-prison experiences of people in prison were characterised by homelessness, unemployment, poor education, mental health issues, being in care and that they came from a minority ethnic background. It concluded:

> Taken as a whole, the 'Identikit Prisoner' is someone who has suffered a range of social and economic disadvantages. A key argument for reducing the use of prison is that, all too often, a period of imprisonment exacerbates those very disadvantages which have led the person into crime in the first place (Prison Reform Trust, 1991: 6).

Today, the same powerless, often-vulnerable people continue to be punished and imprisoned: the unemployed and never employed; the sexually abused; the psychologically traumatized; the homeless; those with drug, alcohol, and mental health issues; people disproportionately excluded from school; and those who have suffered physically traumatic brain injuries. There are also a disproportionate number of individuals who have tried to kill themselves or who have observed domestic violence. Women prisoners are over-represented in the majority of these categories (Prison Reform Trust, 2024: 36). Then there is the 'care-to-prison pipeline'. Although they comprised of less than 1% of the general population, in 2021 children who had been in care made up a quarter of the homeless and prison populations (Ribeiro-Addy, cited in Sim, 2023a: 888). Finally, 'about half of the adult prison population (a "conservative" estimate) experienced some kind of neurodivergence challenge compared with 15–20 percent of the general population' (Bhui, 2024: 90–91).

The prison population is also disproportionality racialised. In 2017, the Lammy Review pointed out that:

> Despite making up just 14% of the population, BAME [Black and Minority Ethnic] men and women make up 25% of prisoners, while over 40% of young people in custody are from BAME backgrounds. If our prison population reflected the make-up of England and Wales, we would have over 9,000 fewer people in prison – the equivalent of 12 average-sized prisons. There is greater disproportionality in the number of Black people in prisons here than in the United States (Lammy Review, 2017: 3).

By 2023, more than 23,000 people – 27% of the ADP – were from an ethnic minority group (Prison Reform Trust, 2024: 40). The percentage was even higher for children. Additionally, just under 10,500 people – 12% of the prison population – were foreign national prisoners (Prison Reform Trust, 2024: 47).

Other examples

The imprisonment of other groups further illustrates the myth about the dangerousness of those inside.

First, there are prisoners on remand. In February 2024, their number was 'at its highest level in at least 50 years'. Nearly 16,200 people – more than one in six of the ADP – were in this category. There were a further 33,971 people remanded to await trial in the year to June 2023. Half of these were accused of non-violent offences. Over 20,000 awaiting sentencing were also remanded in custody (Prison Reform Trust, 2024: 21).

In 2022, 72% of women remanded and tried in magistrates' courts were not given a prison sentence. The equivalent figure for the Crown Court was 48% (Prison Reform Trust, 2024: 49). These figures indicate that 'the vast majority of women remanded to prison to await trial or sentence could safely be released on bail, to the advantage of their families, their communities and the wider criminal justice system' (Howard League for Penal Reform, 2020: no page number). Women on remand can lose their jobs and their homes while their children can be taken into care and experience a 'deep and debilitating sense of loss' (Howard League for Penal Reform, cited in Sim, 2023a: 888) and their life chances can be badly curtailed as a result of their mother's imprisonment (Beresford, cited in Howard League for Penal Reform, cited in Sim, 2023a: 888).

Like every other dimension of the criminal injustice system, being remanded disproportionately impacts on minority ethnic groups: 'Black men [were] 26%, and men with a mixed ethnic background [were] 22% more likely to be remanded in custody at the Crown Court than white men' (Prison Reform Trust, 2023b: 6). The situation for women is even worse: '[f]oreign national and Black, Asian and minority ethnic women are even more likely to be remanded without sufficient reason' (Howard League for Penal Reform, 2020: no page number).

People remanded in custody do not receive financial help from the state when they are released and if they are acquitted they do not receive compensation. In some cases the impact can be even more profound. In 2022, people on remand accounted for 35% of self-inflicted deaths and 16% of self-harm incidents (Prison Reform Trust, 2024: 49).

After Daniel Khalife escaped from Wandsworth in September 2023, the prison was propelled into national headlines. However, the sensationalist accounts of his escape relegated the key issue of the remand population to the margins. In the year to May 2022, out of a population of 1385 in the prison, only 246 were sentenced prisoners. Over half – 734 – were on remand, 197 were immigration detainees and 87 had been recalled to prison (Independent Monitoring Boards, 2023: 6). The state's panic about the escape was such that Wandsworth's Quaker Chaplain was excluded from prisons for five years because she had payed between £15 and £30 into the bank accounts of a small number of prisoners who faced 'destitution and homelessness on their release... '. As she had not informed prison managers of this charitable act, it was decided that the 'payments breached professional standards and posed a security risk to herself and others' (*Private Eye,* 2024a: 38).

There have been significant problems with the remand system for decades which have been ignored by successive governments. In October 1983, in words which could have been written in 2024, the National Association of Probation Officers noted that:

> The high numbers of prisoners on remand is a major contributory factor in prison overcrowding [...] Prisoners on remand are still, in law, presumed innocent, yet conditions inside are often quite appalling. Prisoners share overcrowded cells and are locked up for most of the day. Visits are held in extremely difficult conditions, and those who have jobs and accommodation outside run the risk of losing them (National Association of Probation Officers, 1983: 1–2).

Second, there are those recalled to prison – 9782 between April and June 2024. The majority were recalled *not* because they had committed further offences but for failing to follow the state's often-oppressive rules. During this period, 'about 24% [of recalls] involved a charge of further offending, 77% involved non-compliance, 36% involved failure to keep in touch, and 23% involved failure to reside' (Ministry of Justice, 2024c: Part 5). This group grew from over 6000 in September 2017 to over 12000 in September 2023 (Ministry of Justice, 2024d).

Third, there are those sentenced to Imprisonment for Public Protection (IPP). This scandalous legislation was introduced in 2005 under a previous Labour government. It was a 'life sentence that could be given for any of 153 crimes, including affray and criminal damage. Many of these crimes had never previously been given a life sentence'. In England and Wales, between 2005 and 2013, 8,711 people were given an IPP. In 2012, the sentence was abolished. However, 'it was not abolished retrospectively. On 31st December 2024, 2,614 people were still in prison, serving an IPP sentence' (United Group for Reform of IPP, no date). The impact of this legislation has been devastating.

Thomas White was given a minimum two-year tariff in 2012 for stealing a mobile phone. He had to complete a rehabilitation scheme before being released. However, he had been unable to access a scheme in any of the 16 prisons where he had served time. He was still in prison in 2023, 11 years after he was first sentenced (Gecsoyler, 2023). Tommy Nicol, who killed himself in 2005, was serving an IPP sentence for stealing a car. He was not the only prisoner to kill himself: 'in the 19 years since IPP was introduced, [up to April 2024] 90 prisoners serving the sentence are known to have killed themselves. A 2020 study by the Prison Reform Trust found that IPP prisoners were two and a half times more likely to harm themselves than others in the prison population' (cited in Hattenstone, 2024). The shocking number of deaths were not confined to those inside. Between 2019/20 and 2023/4, 37 IPP prisoners killed themselves in the community (Hansard, 2025). By February 2024:

Nearly three in five unreleased IPP prisoners [had] spent an additional 10 years in prison on top of their original tariff [...] One in 14 [had] served an additional 15 years [...] Over half [...] had an original tariff of less than four years [...] 212 people [had] never been released from prison, despite receiving a tariff of less than two years. Almost every one of them (194 people) [had] served a further ten years or more in addition to their original tariff. There are a further 1,652 people serving an IPP sentence who are back in prison having previously been released – a rise of 14% on the previous year. Recalls now account for more than half the imprisoned IPP population (57%) (Prison Reform Trust, 2024: 18).

In October 2024, five people who had been given minimum terms of less than six months had served more than 16 years. There were another 15 people whose tariff was between six months and a year who had also not been released after 16 years and a further 47 who were in the same category with tariffs of between a year and 18 months (Hansard, 2024a: column 223).

Lastly, there are those sentenced under another scandalous law – Joint Enterprise (JE). This law is based on prosecuting people who might not be the main perpetrators of an offence but who are regarded as encouraging or assisting them. The outcome has been dire: *'bystanders, or people involved in much lesser criminal offences*, [were] being convicted of murder or manslaughter' (Liberty, 2022, emphasis added). The grassroots organization Joint Enterprise Not Guilty by Association (JENGbA) supports approximately 1400 prisoners and their families who are entangled in JE's web (Cunliffe and Morrison, 2023: 492).

This law has differentially impacted on the young and on 'Black people [who] are 16 times more likely than white people to be prosecuted [...] CPS figures show' (Dugan, 2024). It is based on a number of myths about the dangers posed by 'feral', gang-affiliated young people who, for the media, symbolize the idea of 'broken Britain' (Cunliffe and Morrison, 2023: 492):

Individuals can be wrongly charged and convicted when they have been close to a crime, have a random connection with the actual perpetrator via texting or engage in a phone call which is most often used as 'critical evidence'. Many defendants may not even have been at the crime scene but can be convicted of murder by association. More recently, young men, and increasingly young women, have been targeted, where often the sole evidence against them is their choice of music, especially rap or drill music [...] Trials often open with defendants being shown taking part in a video, rapping or making 'gang' signs. This is a signal to the juries that they are criminals before a shred of evidence is produced (Cunliffe and Morrison, 2023: 492).

It is clear from the examples above that prisons, and other state and privately run institutions, are *not* populated with the dangerous, destructive and depraved but with the damaged, destitute and deprived – society's expendable outcasts. And although talking about America, Angela Davis's point is directly relevant to the situation in England and Wales:

Imprisonment has become the response of first resort to far too many of the social problems that burden people who are ensconced in poverty. These problems often are veiled by being conveniently grouped together under the category 'crime' and by the automatic attribution of criminal behaviour to people of colour. Homelessness, unemployment, drug addiction, mental illness, and illiteracy are only a few of the problems that disappear from public view when the human beings contending with them are relegated to cages [...] *prisons do not disappear problems, they disappear human beings*. And the practice of disappearing vast numbers of people from poor, immigrant, and racially marginalized communities has literally become big business (Davis, no date, emphasis added).

Conclusion

Two final cases graphically, and poignantly, illustrate the sheer iniquity and hypocrisy of the criminal injustice system. In 2023, Bernie Ecclestone, the former Chief Executive of the Formula 1 Group, pleaded guilty to tax fraud amounting to £400 million. He received a 17 month suspended sentence. Therefore, 'on a pro rata basis [...] for every £785,000 of any fraud you can only expect a one-day suspended sentence' (Crace, 2023). In 2017, Marie Baker, described as 'fragile and vulnerable', was sentenced to six months. She had been caught begging for 50 pence. Marie could not read or write and had no legal representation as she was unable to receive legal aid (Peat, cited in Sim, 2023a: 887–888). This is how 'justice' is dispensed in England and Wales in the twenty-first century.

Having addressed the myths and misrepresentations about crime and the nature of the prison population, the following chapter considers the myths and misrepresentations about prisons themselves, which are central to the state's unrelenting defence of the institution as a bulwark against crime, deviance and disorder.

what do we know and not know about prisons? myths and misrepresentations

This chapter focuses on a number of myths and misrepresentations around prisons. Not only are they fundamental in the construction of the political and popular 'truth' about prison regimes, which justify the institution's existence and continuous expansion, but also they mystify the grim reality and lived experiences of people in prison. At the same time, they reinforce the misguided and ultimately false claim that if Armageddon is to be avoided then prisons are essential for maintaining law and order. However, this begs the question 'whose law and what order'? (Chambliss and Mankoff, 1976).

Prisons are 'holiday camps'

The idea that the prison is a 'holiday camp' is a widely disseminated myth. Spending on prisoners' food alone challenges this myth. In 2023/24, prisons were allocated £2.70 per prisoner per day for meals, a *rise* of 25% from the previous year (*Inside Time*, 2023). The conditions and regimes in many prisons also challenge this myth. People in prison are human junk left to fester in rotting and rotten penal dustbins which are demoralising, dehumanising, degrading and mortifying. For decades, the Prison Inspectorate, and other official bodies, have published a series of withering reports which bear witness to these conditions. In 2018, communal areas in Birmingham prison:

> […] in most wings were filthy. Rubbish had accumulated and had not been removed. There were widespread problems with insects, including cockroaches, as well as rats and other vermin. We saw evidence of bodily fluids left unattended, including blood and vomit. I saw a shower area where there was bloodstained clothing and a pool of blood that apparently had been there for two days next to numerous rat droppings. Many cells were cramped, poorly equipped and had damaged flooring or plasterwork. Most toilets were poorly screened, many were leaking and we saw cells with exposed electrics (The Prison Inspectorate, cited in Sim, 2018a).

In their annual report for 2017/18, the Independent Monitoring Boards who monitor prisons and immigration detention centres noted that in 'nearly all' of the annual reports from Boards at different prisons, the situation was:

> […] extremely depressing, with failures, sometimes compromising health and safety, across all kinds of prison and in all areas. Four boards described conditions as 'squalid'; others as inhumane and unfit for purpose […] At Lincoln, the Health and Safety Executive is still investigating the origin of a legionella outbreak that left one prisoner dead. Nearly all open prisons reported major problems, with some accommodation that was barely fit for purpose (Independent Monitoring Boards, 2019: 19).

In 2019, a 71-year-old prisoner in Wormwood Scrubs, who suffered from nightmares and depression, sued the prison service for post-traumatic stress disorder after he complained about rats running across his body. He was told that the prison was not 'a hotel, you know. *You're here to be punished*' (cited in Taylor, 2019, emphasis added). By 2022, conditions had not improved elsewhere:

[...] at Chelmsford, for example, this was a longstanding and apparently intractable issue: 'There is still an infestation of rats... rats run freely in the wings, even climbing the stairs. Live and dead rats have been found in serveries, and dead rats have been found in exercise yards. The rodents also chewed through cabling, disabling phone systems in the process. This situation is clearly unacceptable' (Independent Monitoring Boards, 2022a: 15).

In September 2023, a German court refused to extradite a prisoner to Britain because of the state of the prisons (Taylor, 2023b). In November, the Chief Inspector of Prisons wrote to the Justice Secretary about the putrid state of Bedford:

New prisoners were placed into dirty, graffitied cells and were given a very limited induction – of particular concern in a reception prison [...] Three-quarters of the prisoners lived in overcrowded conditions. Most spent more than 22 hours a day locked in their cells. The wings were dirty and there was a widespread infestation of rats and cockroaches. Some cells had broken windows and black mould on the walls. The segregation unit was squalid, staff were forced to use sandbags and wear wellington boots due to overflowing sewage pipes after heavy rain (Taylor, 2023: 1).

In early 2024, the Inspectorate published another damning report on the same prison:

[...] standards of cleanliness on wings and in cells had worsened considerably since our last inspection. On this visit we found filthy floors and serveries that compounded the overcrowded conditions in which most prisoners were held, while many cells had broken furniture [and] windows and were covered [in] graffiti [...] Some of the accommodation in Bedford was the worst I have seen. On E wing, the smell of mould in one cell was overpowering, with the walls damp to the touch, while the underground segregation unit was a disgrace [...] on very wet days, raw sewage covered the floor and the cells were dark, damp and dilapidated [...] There was a widespread infestation of rats, cockroaches and pigeons (HM Inspectorate of Prisons, 2024a: 3 and 27).

By the end of the year, the dire circle was complete with yet another damning report from the Independent Monitoring Boards concerning the inhumane conditions in many prisons. The report identified rat and cockroach infestations, broken windows and sewage spills. People in prison were:

[...] enduring appalling conditions across the board, yet they often lack the motivation to submit complaints, as the dire state of things has become normalised for those most affected. Whether they are eating, working, sleeping, or receiving medical care, the shocking level of neglect reported by local IMBs across the country, and the impact of this on those living in these conditions, cannot be ignored (Independent Monitoring Boards, 2024a).

Overall, as of October 2024, the reports by the Independent Monitoring Boards indicated that '29% of 120 prisons had serious maintenance issues, dilapidated or poor building conditions or inhumane environments [...] Almost 26,000 prisoners were being held in one of these prisons...' This in turn, had an impact on rehabilitation such as at Elmley prison where the 'poor experience of prison accommodation is unlikely to benefit any attempts at rehabilitation' (Goodier, 2024).

Ultimately, the seemingly endless flow of reports, even from official bodies, undermine the claim that prisons are 'holiday camps'. In fact, the reverse is the case. These institutions are harm-inducing which, as illustrated below, break the spirit and psyches of many people inside.

Prisons are an effective way of responding to violence and keeping communities safe

It is claimed that prisons protect individuals and communities from dangerous individuals. However, this too is a myth. As the prison abolitionist Ruth Morris has argued, '[the] greatest fraud perpetrated by our retributive justice system is that it exists to protect us from the dangerous few' (cited in Whynacht, 2021: 26). What constitutes this fraud?

First, there is the question of definition. Who defines which individuals and what actions are dangerous? Who defines which individuals and what actions are not dangerous? And, crucially, who defines which individuals, and what actions, have the most socially harmful impact?

Take deaths due to homicides. There were 590 in England and Wales in the year ending March 2023 (Office for National Statistics, 2024a). It is indisputable that the deep pain, intense trauma and grievous sense of loss experienced by the friends and families of the deceased should be recognised. At the same time, as Chapter 1 noted, powerful individuals also engage in actions and non-actions, nationally and internationally, which cause hundreds of thousands of preventable deaths each year, which bring an enormous sense of loss and trauma to the families and friends of the dead and which are effectively ignored. These deaths are generated by: state violence; genocide; poverty and destitution; homelessness; hunger and malnutrition; food poisoning; ageism; disablism, medical negligence and delays in medical care; air pollution; environmental degradation; legally prescribed drugs; corruption; misogynistic, racist and homophobic violence; the systemic failure to enforce health and safety laws in the workplace and children dying – at least 74 in England, one a month since 2020 – from a combination of homelessness and living accommodation consisting of overcrowding, mould and a lack of cots and

Moses baskets (Scott and Sim, 2023: 31–32; Welsh and Puri, 2025). It is also worth noting that cuts to environmental and health protection agencies, legitimated by the anti-regulation discourse of neoliberalism, have also contributed to the removal of a range of 'social protection' measures resulting in preventable social harms, including deaths (Tombs, 2016a).

So while prisons incapacitate people convicted of legally-defined murder, those whose actions and non-actions cause hundreds of thousands of preventable deaths literally get away with murder, in this case 'social murder' which has been defined in the following terms:

> When one individual inflicts bodily injury upon another such injury that death results, we call the deed manslaughter; when the assailant knew in advance that the injury would be fatal, we call his [sic] deed murder. But when society places hundreds of proletarians in such a position that they inevitably meet a too early and an unnatural death, one which is quite as much a death by violence as that by the sword or bullet; when it deprives thousands of the necessaries of life, places them under conditions in which they cannot live – forces them, through the strong arm of the law, to remain in such conditions until that death ensues which is the inevitable consequence – knows that these thousands of victims must perish, and yet permits these conditions to remain, its deed is murder just as surely as the deed of the single individual (Engels, cited in Grover, 2019).

For Chris Grover, cuts to the benefits system have generated 'social murder by destitution'. This included homeless people dying on the streets and in temporary accommodation; deaths due to malnutrition as well as those caused by the spiralling cost of heating homes which were already inadequately insulated. In other words, there is a 'long-standing association between poor material conditions and social murder' (Grover, 2019).

Grover's point about social murder and destitution is also reflected in the data concerning excess deaths involving cuts to public services and benefits in England, Wales and Scotland. It has been estimated that between 2012 and 2019 there were over 334,000 excess deaths associated with these cuts (cited in Butler, 2022). And while the number of deaths in this category are not all preventable, their sheer extent also points to the relationship between social murder and the 'dismembering of the state', in this case the welfare state (Toynbee and Walker, 2017).

Second, the myths and misrepresentations around dangerousness lead to another question: do prisons actually prevent violence and social harm? The answer is no. The relentless extent of male violence against women and girls provides a powerful case study of the relationship, or lack of relationship, between prisons and reducing the dangers women and girls face on a daily basis. Even on its own terms, the state's response to this violence has been nothing short of abysmal. After the murder of Quyen Ngoc Nguyen, whose killer was on probation, the system for protecting women was described by an inquest jury as 'dysfunctional'. In Lisa Skidmore's case, her killer told the police and the probation service that he was a danger to women. No action was taken and this contributed to Lisa's murder (Atkinson et al, 2023: 203).

Furthermore, between October 2022 and September 2023, 67,398 rapes were recorded by the police. Charges were brought in 1631 (2.4%) cases, just 2 in 100. In the year ending March 2022, 798,000 or 1 in 30 women, were raped or sexually assaulted (Rape Crisis England and Wales, no date). At the same time, only 'marginal progress' was being made in prosecutions for rape while 'the number of convictions [...] remain[ed] far from 2016 levels' (End Violence Against Women, 2023).

These deplorable figures illustrate a key point about dangerousness made by Victoria Law. Arresting, prosecuting and imprisoning the few men convicted of sexual violence happens 'only *after* harm or violence has occurred. Incarceration does not prevent these acts from happening' (Law, 2021: 132, original emphasis). The same can be said of murder. What Law terms 'the criminal legal system' (Law, 2021: vii) intervenes 'only *after* harm or violence has occurred. It does not prevent people from causing harm' (Law, 2021: 136, original emphasis). America provides a compelling example of this point. Put simply, 'if all arrested Americans were a nation, they would be the world's eighteenth largest... Holding hands, [they] could circle the earth three times' (Brennan Centre for Justice cited in Wypijewski, 2024). And yet:

Again and again we see that incarceration does not prevent rape or murder. If it did, the US would have the world's lowest rates of sexual assault and murder since it has the highest rate of incarceration. But given the low rates of reporting, investigating, prosecuting and imprisoning, we see that's not the case. Instead, our reliance on prisons lulls us into ignoring the social, cultural, and economic factors that lead to violence *and ultimately make us less safe* [...] How can we respond to violence in ways that not only address the current incident[s] of violence, but also help to transform the conditions that allowed it to happen? (Law, 2021: 140 and 174, emphasis added).

Pointing to this issue does *not* mean that men convicted of violence against women and girls should be able to walk the streets, irrespective of what they have done. This is an offensive myth and misrepresentation that is often attributed to prison abolitionists, as Chapter 5 illustrates. Therefore, it is necessary to recognise that 'there are some incarcerated people who are tremendously dangerous to our individual and collective safety' (Whynacht, 2021: 29). However, for Law, this raises another key issue:

[...] we can banish those who commit harm without asking questions about why they harmed in the first place... [A] refusal to acknowledge the causes of violence allows us to scapegoat individuals for forms of violence that are taught and maintained in everyday life (Law, 2021: 118).

In other words, a 'system that never addresses the *why* behind a harm never actually contains the harm itself' (Kaba, cited in Law, 2021: 118, original emphasis).

Finally, incarcerating violent men in institutions which are heavily and intensely masculine is also, in itself, problematic. Their misogynistic attitudes and behaviour are more likely to be reinforced than challenged in these places. Nor does imprisoning them deal with the structural, deeply embedded relationship between masculinity and the exercise of patriarchal power. This goes to the heart of Mariame Kaba's point above about not asking the 'why' question, in this case about the normalisation and reproduction of male violence on a daily basis, inside and outside prisons through the praxis of hegemonic masculinity. The prison mystifies the why question and, ideologically, reproduces the dominant narrative that male violence is the preserve of individual 'monsters' rather than a widespread, structural, normal pattern of behaviour which demeans and destroys the everyday lives of many women and girls and for which the prison has no answer. In fact, defenders of the institution are not even asking the why question with respect to this violence.

Prisons are safe places for people in prison

As Chapter 3 noted, in general, people in prison are not dangerous. However; prisons *are* dangerous for them. This point has been made not only by prison abolitionists but also by the Prison Inspectorate. In the case of Nottingham prison, '[f]or too long prisoners have been held in a *dangerous,* disrespectful, drug-ridden jail. My fear, which may prove to be unfounded, is that some could face it no longer and took their own lives' (HM Inspectorate of Prisons, 2018a: 7, emphasis added).

Prisons break many of those who are already broken. They generate a 'spirit of death' – corporeal, civil, social, spiritual, emotional and psychological (Scott, 2018: 163). This 'spirit of death' is psychologically profound in that it denies people in prison hope for a better future: '[s]uch a loss of hope in the future can prove deadly' (Scott and Codd, cited in Scott, 2018: 164). The devastating levels of death and self-harm inside, and outside, amongst people under community supervision, also illustrates the dangerous lack of safety in their lives. In 2015, there were:

[...] ten times more self-inflicted deaths per 1000 people in custody than there were suicides per 1000 people in the community. Men in prison were six times more likely to take their own life than men in the community, and women in prison were 24 times more likely to take their own life than women in the community (National Audit Office, cited in Atkinson et al, 2023: 200).

In 2018, the average age of people dying in prison in England was 56, while the death rate for those who had been in prison and those serving community sentences was 'even higher than that of the prison population...' (House of Commons Health and Social Care Committee, 2018: 13). In the 12 months to December 2023, 311 people died inside, up 3% from the previous 12 months. Ninety three of these deaths were self-inflicted, up 22% in the same period. There were a further 179 deaths from 'natural causes' (Ministry of Justice, 2024e). However, for the charity INQUEST, the state's claim that people die 'natural' deaths in prison is wrong: 'many of these deaths are premature and far from "natural"' (INQUEST, 2022a).

Women in prison face specific health and safety issues which are *not* generated by other prisoners but arise from the state's failure to fulfil its duty of care towards them. The self-inflicted death of Christine McDonald, a 55-year-old parent to four children, brutally highlights this issue. Christine died in Styal prison in 2019 – the fact that it took five years for the inquest to take place is a scandal in itself. She had been sentenced to 12 weeks for shoplifting shampoo, bubble bath, hair dye and cheese to fund her opiate addiction and for failing to comply with the community requirement of a suspended sentence. There had been 26 deaths in the prison since 2007, 11 of which were self-inflicted. At her inquest, the jury found there was 'a gross failure to provide care and attention to Christine that directly contributed to her death'. A number of factors were involved:

- Christine had used her cell bell to ask to see a nurse shortly before she ligatured
- The prison officer did not action the request

- Christine should have been assessed by healthcare on her return from hospital but was not
- The message in relation to the well-being of Christine's daughter should have been communicated to Christine but was not
- There was a failure by healthcare to follow the clinical guidance about the assessment and treatment of Christine's drug dependency
- There were failings in communications between healthcare staff and prison staff at HMP Styal (INQUEST, 2024b).

For pregnant women, the danger can be acute. Rianna Cleary, who was 18 and pregnant, spent more than 12 hours alone in labour in the privately run Bronzefield prison, the biggest women's prison in Europe, and the country's most expensive to run. Rianna had repeatedly pressed her cell bell for help. When it arrived, 'she was covered in blood with her dead baby [Aisha]. She had bitten through the umbilical cord as she had no other way to sever it' (Taylor, 2024).

The appalling levels of self-harm provide one, final illustration of the issues around women's health and safety, or the lack of it, inside. In the 12 months to September 2023, there were nearly 68,000 incidents – over 7 an hour. There were 5988 incidents per 1000 prisoners, more than 10 times the rate in men's prisons (Ministry of Justice, 2024e). These figures, and the deaths discussed above, clearly illustrate that imprisoning women does more harm than good and should be understood as 'a form of state sanctioned violence... and part of a cycle of harm that too often leads to trauma, injury and death. The use of punishment and imprisonment is the result of a lack of political will to take seriously violence against women across society' (INQUEST, 2018: 19, original emphasis).

Then there are the deaths of racialised people in prison which occur in the context of a system based on 'institutional racism' (INQUEST, 2022b: 6). They experience regimes which disproportionately impact on them including: the inappropriate use of segregation, racial stereotyping, a hostile environment, the neglect of their physical and mental health, the failure to respond to warning signs and bullying and victimisation

(INQUEST, 2022b: 62-68). Wayne Bayley's death in 2022 crystallised a number of these issues. Wayne, a Black, 43-year-old remand prisoner, had been diagnosed with sickle cell disease, epilepsy and delusional disorder. Before he died, he had been restrained by staff. In October 2024, an inquest jury found that he had died of:

> [...] acute chest syndrome – the most common fatal complication of sickle cell disease – caused by the restraint [...] While being conveyed under restraint to the segregation unit, he collapsed to his knees and told officers that he could not breathe. Despite this, Wayne was subject to a forcible strip search in which his clothes were cut off him and he was left naked in a segregation cell. The nurse responsible for monitoring his physical health during and after the restraint failed to address his stark deterioration [...] After seven hours in segregation, Wayne was conveyed to the prison's healthcare for a mental health assessment. On the way, Wayne was so frail he collapsed to his knees and had to be transported in a wheelchair. On arrival, despite telling healthcare staff he could not breathe and asking to see a doctor, vital observations were again not taken in breach of protocol and no other care was rendered [...] The jury found a litany of failures that caused Wayne's death [and] was contributed to by neglect (INQUEST, 2024c).

People with cancer in prison are more likely to die from the disease than those in the general population. They are 28% less likely to receive treatment, particularly surgery that removes tumours and they have a '9% increased risk of death – half of which is due to treatment differences' (Bawden, 2024). For one commentator:

> [...] these findings only represent part of a broken system where the healthcare needs of prisoners are systematically and regularly not being met. Prisoners should have the same right and access to healthcare services as everyone else, but this basic premise is far from reality (cited in Bawden, 2024).

The Prisons Inspectorate has also examined the experiences of immigration detainees held in prison and found that they were '"substantially disadvantaged" compared to those held in immigration removal centres, and that detention adversely affect[ed] their welfare' (cited in Prison Reform Trust, 2024: 47). Between 2000 and January 2024, there were 16 deaths of people in this group who were held in prison, 13 of which were self-inflicted (INQUEST, 2024a). The Inspectorate has warned that the safety of those held in immigration removal centres, such as Harmondsworth and Yarl's Wood, was deteriorating and was traumatising 'vulnerable migrants' (cited in Kersley, 2024). The charity Medical Justice has described these institutions as 'dangerous' for the often vulnerable and traumatised people they detain (cited in PA Media, 2024).

In 2017, an undercover investigation by BBC's Panorama programme 'portrayed Brook House [immigration removal centre] as violent, dysfunctional and unsafe. It showed the use of abusive, racist and derogatory language by some staff towards those in their care, the effects of illicit drugs, and the use of force by staff on mentally and physically unwell detained people' (Eves, 2023: 1–2). A public inquiry endorsed the programme's findings, although why it took a television programme, and an official inquiry, to bring this to the state's attention is another issue. The inquiry found appalling levels of violence, degradation, humiliation and the use of force, while staff made 'inappropriate and humiliating comments' towards two prisoners 'as they were attempting to take their own lives' (Eves, 2023: 4). For the inquiry's Chair:

> One of the most shocking incidents I considered, which was central to the Panorama programme, was the moment Detention Custody Officer (DCO) Ioannis (Yan) Paschali placed his hands firmly around the neck of one detained person (referred to by the Inquiry as D1527), leaned forward over him and said in a quiet voice: 'You fucking piece of shit, because I'm going to put you to fucking sleep' (Eves, 2023: 3).

As noted above, people newly released from prison also face danger and death. After investigating 137 cases, the Prisons and Probation

Ombudsman (PPO) found that just over half died within four days of being released. Drugs and homelessness were involved in these deaths with the latter being a 'considerable issue'. The PPO argued that it was:

> […] critical that prisoners are released to safe and suitable accommodation with early access to and engagement with substance misuse services […] On reviewing the 105 post-release death reports we repeatedly saw that being released homeless has a detrimental impact on the individuals involved […] Our investigations found instances where staff did not make the correct referrals, made the referrals too late or did not communicate key information to the prisoner about their accommodation (Prisons and Probation Ombudsman, 2024: 8 and 9).

Prisons are dangerous to the health of people in prison in other ways. When Olney prison was inspected in 2019, it was described as 'funda-mentally unsafe'. One in six prisoners 'had acquired a drug habit *inside* the prison'. David Richardson died a month after he was released from Birmingham prison. David had become addicted to spice in prison and was 'knocked down by a car on a busy dual carriageway while under the influence of drugs' (Acheson, 2024: 65 and 217, original emphasis).

The toxic nature of the majority of prison regimes severely compro-mises the psychological and physical health and safety of people inside making *all* of them potentially vulnerable to experiencing a 'natural' or self-inflicted death – what Dorling has described more broadly as 'death[s] of despair' (Dorling, 2024: 235) or engaging in self-harm. The state's focus is on vulnerable prisoners who, it is claimed, are at risk. By implication, if these prisoners could be 'scientifically' identified, then the number of deaths would be reduced. This individualises the problem and distracts attention from the structural and institutionalised failures behind the deaths inside. Furthermore, and contrary to what state agents and media 'experts' argue, in prisons where deaths and self-harm do occur, the regimes are *not* out of control. They are *in* control of the people inside, revving up fears and anxieties to unacceptable and unbearable levels while brutally extinguishing their individual hopes and desires to change for the better. Their aching desolation is ignored. An institutionalised taboo on compassion, mercy and empathy prevails, leaving no circle of safety for them.

People in prison are a danger to the health and safety of staff

Those who present an alternative perspective to the dominant narrative about the dangers prison staff face are often offensively labelled as supporting violence against them. This is not the case. What they *are* concerned about is establishing the reality of the claims made about these dangers including critically analysing the statistics which underpin claims such as those made by the Prison Officers Association (POA) that prisons are 'the most violent workplace in Europe' (cited in Acheson, 2024: 13).

One way to critically investigate this assertion would be to compare the deaths and injuries sustained by prison staff with those sustained by staff in other occupations. However, in the 108 occupational categories used by the Health and Safety Executive, there is no separate category for prison (or police) officers in order to make this comparison (Health and Safety Executive, 2024). What *is* known is that eight members of staff, not all of them prison officers, died between 1850 and 2018. During that period, the last murder occurred in 1965 (Scott, 2018: 155). To be clear, this is *not* to dismiss the deaths of prison staff but it is to put the dangers staff face into context.

Assaults are another area where it is claimed that the health and safety of staff is compromised. Implicitly and explicitly, prisoners are assumed to be violent. However, the Chief Inspector of Prisons noted that at Eastwood Park women's prison:

> [...] most assaults were minor and some incidents against staff had been recorded inaccurately, as they had not been actual assaults,

which made the levels of violence appear much higher than they actually were (HM Inspectorate of Prisons, 2019: 22, emphasis added).

Focussing on assaults also ignores another key point concerning the 'many examples of prisoners going to the aid of officers in dangerous situations rather than using violence against them' (Scott, 2018: 155).

As ever, the media has been pivotal in amplifying and overdramatising the nature and extent of the assaults to the detriment of *actually* exploring the reality on the ground. In response to a scathing Prisons Inspectorate report on Birmingham prison, *Channel 4 News* interviewed a member of staff:

> Answering the presenter's extraordinarily leading question 'Do you feel safe, do your colleagues feel safe?' a serving prison officer replied that ex-military personnel working in British prisons *said they felt safer in Afghanistan and Iraq* (cited in Sim, 2018a, emphasis added).

There is little data about the number of convictions arising from assaults on staff. This is important as court proceedings allow evidence to be tested to establish guilt or innocence. In 2022, the Independent Monitoring Board at Wandsworth *did* provide data, which, as ever, received scant media coverage. While being 'very concerned' about the 'deteriorating situation' about assaults on staff, the Board noted that:

> The focus on referring serious assaults to the police continued, despite the difficulty in achieving positive, timely outcomes. During the period *only one* (2020/21: two) assault on a member of staff referred to the police in the prior period led to a conviction. Of 371 further cases referred to the police during the period, *only 17* were passed to the Crown Prosecution Service (CPS) (Independent Monitoring Boards, 2022b: 19, emphasis added).

Continually focusing on the assaults that *do* occur distorts the reality of the everyday working lives of staff and distracts attention from the structural generators of ill-health which result in many more days being lost at work compared with the number of days lost due to assaults. The challenge to their health and safety is caused, *not* by prisoners, but by working in an environment which generates musculoskeletal problems, anxiety, depression and stress, often caused by management. These structural dimensions are systematically ignored while assaults are overdramatised in terms of their seriousness (Sim, 2004).

In November 2024, coincidently, or perhaps not, in the same week that it was revealed that a record number of prison officers had been sacked in the course of a year – 165 or nearly 1 every 3 days (Kotecha, 2024) – the *Observer* newspaper, heavily quoting serving and ex-staff, published another report under the sensationalist headline – 'More than a third of assaults on UK prison officers are not fully investigated' (Smith, 2024). Leaving aside the fact that around two thirds of assaults on staff *were* investigated, and that by far the biggest reported increase involved sexual assaults, which raised serious questions once again about the politics of masculinity in prisons but which the report also ignored, it made the unreferenced claim that 'assaults against staff in prisons have almost tripled since 2005' (Smith, 2024). The issue had come full circle, the ventriloquists at the POA had, once again, found a faithful media dummy. It is also worth pointing out that if 165 social workers or probation officers had been sacked in a year, arguably there would have been endless comments from politicians and uproar in the media. However, in the case of prison officer criminality, the prevailing mood was political and media silence.

State violence against people in prison is rare

What about state violence *against* people in prison? Compared with violence against staff, this issue receives little media coverage or political attention. It is also surrounded by a series of myths and misrepresentations, not least of which is the state's claim that it is both rare and is due to the actions of the odd 'bad apple' working on the landings. However, the 'bad apple' discourse has been challenged. Prison abolitionists would argue that it is not the individual prison officer that is the problem. Rather, the issue is the occupational culture of prison staff built on systemic coercion, corrosive masculinity, the discretionary use of often, non-accountable power, institutionalised indifference and moral opprobrium directed towards people in prison (Sim, 2009).

This violence 'remains shrouded in silence and "literal denial" […] There has consistently been a failure to acknowledge that prison officer violence happens at all, and certainly not at a systemic level' (Scott, 2020a: 98). Importantly, it has been highlighted by prisoners *and* by prison staff: 'there are […] detailed accounts of prison officer violence in prison officer auto-biographies. Prison officers have almost universally in their accounts of their prison working lives written about the perpetration of physical violence against prisoners by themselves or other officers' (Scott, 2020b). This important point is also reflected in comments made by Martin Narey, the former Director General of the Prison Service, who started his career as a prison officer in Lincoln prison. In the segregation unit, he observed:

> prisoners […] routinely slapped, it was constant low-level abuse. If you wanted to do any good, you had to do it by stealth. The […] Prison Officers Association […] ran the place. Assistant governors were derided. I can remember getting a real load of abuse for being seen carrying a *Guardian* (cited in Sim, 2009: 147).

How this violence is recorded, or *not* recorded, is another issue. In 2018, the Prisons Inspectorate pointed out that the use of force against prisoners in Liverpool, Nottingham and Exeter prisons was not adequately recorded (Sim, 2018b; Sim, 2018c). In April 2020, a delegation from the European Committee for the Prevention of Torture (CPT) investigated three male prisons – Liverpool, Wormwood Scrubs and Doncaster – and noted that in the first two prisons, the delegation:

> […] encountered examples of the unprovoked and unjustified infliction of violence on prisoners by staff […] the use of force paperwork at Liverpool Prison produced by prison staff could be

inaccurate and misleading, and examined more deeply eleven other cases, in which there could have been instances of unprovoked attacks by prison staff on inmates being qualified as 'preventive/ protective strikes'. These included cases in which prisoners had apparently sustained injuries after direct contact with prison officers and had made complaints about ill treatment. In the course of follow-up interviews with certain of the prisoners concerned, the delegation received several further allegations concerning violence by staff on prisoners (Council of Europe, 2020: 22–23).

In the year to May 2023, Wandsworth's Independent Monitoring Board pointed out that force was used against prisoners over 2200 times, an increase of 49% (Independent Monitoring Boards, 2023: 14). In other words, force was used just over six times a day, or once every four hours. Prisoners from minority ethnic backgrounds were particularly impacted in different prisons:

In one prison, white staff told us that Black prisoners were more likely to be loud and boisterous, leading to staff feeling threatened and being quicker to use force against them. Among staff more generally, there was a strong tendency to talk about Black prisoners in terms of threat (HM Inspectorate of Prisons, 2022a: 41).

The Wormwood Scrubs Board also found that while 'Black/Black British prisoners' constituted 27% of the prison's population, they were involved in 43% of Use of Force (UoF) incidents:

There were 856 UoF incidents (657 last year), with an average monthly figure of 71 (range: 57 to 97). Broken down by ethnicity, recorded incidents over the period show a disproportionate number by population involving Black/Black British prisoners, as they did last year (Independent Monitoring Boards, 2024b: 12).

In April 2025, leaked messages from Parc prison revealed that a member of staff responded to a prisoner's complaint by arguing that prisoners needed 'to be broken mentally and physically' (Kotecha, 2025). In an exchange concerning another prisoner:

> 'XXX opened the door and they smashed him into the shower lol.' A response to the message said: 'Good! I hope they hurt him too.' A separate exchange used an expletive to describe punching an inmate 'after he bit me so there's some closure', along with a laughing emoji. Other messages included jokes about someone who was said to be at risk of taking their life and another offender who was seriously self-harming (Kotecha, 2025).

Gathering evidence about the use of force through utilising Body Worn Video Cameras (BWVCs) was problematic. This was due to the reluctance of staff to deploy them. When they were taken up after being pushed by governors at the prison, their deployment was restricted. Their use 'rapidly slid back once attention [was] diverted' (Independent Monitoring Boards, 2024b: 12).

In Garth prison, their implementation was 'too low. Important evidence showing the justification for using force and attempts at de-escalation was not, therefore, routinely recorded' (HM Inspectorate of Prisons, 2022b: 5). The Prisons and Probation Ombudsman made a similar point. Their annual reports made 'repeated recommendations' about how the use of force was investigated due to the failure to switch on BWVCs and retain CCTV footage (Prisons and Probation Ombudsman, 2022: 34).

Unofficial and illegal punishments are also used by staff, a point which once again, people in prison *and* prison staff have been making for centuries (Scott, 2020a). In Liverpool, prisoners who refused to leave the segregation unit were subjected to sanctions which 'lacked decency such as withholding showers and telephone calls'. Crucially, these sanctions were 'applied by staff outside of any formal policy' and, therefore, 'constituted unofficial punishment'. The use of force was barely documented by prison staff while unexplained injuries 'were recorded but not investigated' (HM Prison Inspectorate, cited in Sim, 2018b).

The current prison crisis is largely generated by underfunding

For the Prison Officers Association, and the majority of politicians and media commentators, the cause of the current crisis lies squarely at the door of the Conservative/Liberal government and the brutal cuts imposed on the public sector from 2010. Between 2008 and 2018, the Ministry of Justice's operating budget was cut by 27%. This compared with cuts of 5% and 6% in the Education and Defence budgets respectively (Acheson, 2024: 74).

The impact on staff numbers has become central to the debate about the crisis. In 2014, the Howard League for Penal Reform argued that 'the combination of fewer prison officers, fewer cells and more prisoners has created a severely understaffed and overcrowded prison system which is now at breaking point' (Howard League for Penal Reform, 2014). For some, the state's response to the cuts through encouraging voluntary redundancies has only exacerbated the crisis: '[t]he net effect of this policy was to remove about 70,000 years of experience from prison landings and not replace them with anything' (Acheson, 2024: 74). It is claimed that restoring staff numbers and the prison budget to their pre-2010 levels will solve the crisis. By implication, this will allow prisons to return to their principle goal – the rehabilitation of people inside. There are a number of problems with this argument.

The crisis generated by the cuts was *not* a new phenomenon and did *not* begin in 2010. As Chapter 2 illustrated, not only have prisons been in crisis for two hundred years but the pre-cuts era was rarely, if ever, based on rehabilitation. The cuts have *intensified* the systemic problems which were already deeply embedded in the system. Returning prisons *back* to their normal, operational levels will not solve these systemic problems. Two examples illustrate this point.

In 2018, the Prisons Inspectorate highlighted the dire state of a number of prisons, including Exeter. Staff numbers were *not* an issue in this prison. Nonetheless, those inside still suffered:

In the context of a prison with significant levels of vulnerability among prisoners, and where suicide and self-harm are at such high levels, it was shocking to see the way in which cell call bells were routinely ignored by staff. Given that the prison is now *much better staffed, this was inexcusable.* Inspectors saw bells going unanswered *even when staff were doing nothing else.* Even on the first night and induction landings, where prisoners are likely to be at their most vulnerable, bells were left unanswered for long periods. The prison's own recording system showed that it was commonplace for bells not to be answered within a reasonable time. The system was either not being reviewed by managers, or what it revealed was being ignored (HM Inspectorate of Prisons, 2018b, emphasis added).

For Rory Stewart, the former prisons minister, restoring the prison budget did not defuse the crisis when he was in post. As he pointedly noted: '[,,] even now that the cuts had ceased, and more money and staff were returning, prisons were still getting filthier, *more drug ridden, violent and out of control by the day'* (Stewart, 2023: 275, emphasis added).

Second, there is the question of preventable prison deaths referred to above. These deaths have occurred since prisons first emerged at the end of the eighteenth century as sites for delivering punishment and pain (Sim, 1990). In Wandsworth, between 1978 and 2010, *the pre-cuts era,* there were 118 deaths, 54 of which were self-inflicted (Ministry of Justice, no date). In other words, in the pre-cuts era, 'normal' prison regimes generated terrible social harms and were *not* sites of rehabilitation as the defenders of the system claim.

The harms of the prison are *not* the result of cuts but *are* intrinsic to the very structure, culture and practices of the institution and have been present for centuries. And even if the state returned to the pre-cuts, fully staffed, well-funded, 'benevolent' penal, status quo, the small number of lawbreakers who are caught and processed, will continue to experience pain, punishment, trauma and systemic, state indifference towards them.

What about prison expenditure? According to the Institute for Government:

Following deep cuts in the first half of the 2010s, prisons spending increased from 2015/16. The trend continued in the first year of the pandemic, with spending rising by 5.1% in 2020/21, before falling by 4.3% to £3.7bn in 2021/22 as Covid support measures ended. Following the 2022 autumn statement and current inflation forecasts, spending is expected to increase in real terms by 1.6% in 2023/24, leaving spending 1.7% below 2009/10 levels (Richards and Davies, 2023).

While recognising that cuts have occurred, there is another question that is rarely, if ever, asked. How is funding for prisons, and for law and order 'services' more generally, distributed? Put bluntly, where does the money go? This question is pertinent given that expenditure in both areas is still high, despite the cuts. Between 2015/16 and 2019/20, prison expenditure was over £18 billion while nearly £122 billion was spent in England alone on public order and safety. This amounted to £463 per head of the population in the latter year. In contrast, spending on housing was £180 per head, on environmental protection £162 and on recreation, culture and religion £100 (HM Treasury, cited in Sim, 2023a: 895). In 2022–23, the average cost of a prison place was over £51,000 (Ministry of Justice, 2024f). What has the state's largesse achieved in ensuring that the prison fulfils its official goals in rehabilitating people in prison, reducing reoffending, and generating a genuine sense of individual safety and a general culture of protection? The answer is very little. On its own terms, the uncritical funding of prisons has been a dismal failure.

Building more and 'better' prisons will solve the crisis

For decades, building new prisons has been *the* state response to successive prison crises. It is claimed that new prisons, alongside more investment, will defuse the crisis and allow the institution to fulfill its official goals. However, this is another myth and misrepresentation and is exemplified by the prison building programme announced in October 1983, by Leon Brittan, the new Home Secretary in Margaret Thatcher's second Conservative government. It was, he said, the biggest prison building programme of the twentieth century comprising of 14 new prisons, refurbishing existing institutions and employing 5000 new staff. Achieving parole was to be made more difficult for certain categories of offenders, life sentence prisoners were to remain in prison until the Home Secretary sanctioned their release and minimum sentences of 20 years were to be introduced for those who murdered a police or prison officer or who used firearms in robberies. Sentences designated as over-lenient were to be referred back to the Court of Appeal (Ryan and Sim, 1984). The Home Secretary's authoritarian strategy was not surprising. It was formulated in the context of a series of more general policy developments which saw an intensification in the state's power to target the behaviour of the poor and the powerless, while ignoring the crimes committed by the powerful (Sim, 2009).

What did these changes actually achieve? Did more prisons deliver their intended goals? By November 1986, the answer to this question was clear. The 'big expenditure on new prisons' was described as a '"costly failure"'. Citing the National Association for the Care and Resettlement of Offenders, Peter Evans noted in *The Times* that between March 1981 and March 1985 there had been no reduction in prison crowding (Evans, 1986: 5). Forty years after this building programme, 74 out of 122 prisons (61%) were crowded. This involved more than one fifth of the prison population, a situation which had 'remained broadly unchanged for the last 19 years' (Prison Reform Trust, 2023c: 23).

The myth that building more prisons is a panacea for ending the succession of systemic crises is reinforced by another myth. It is claimed that 'modernising' prisons through new designs will alleviate the situation inside and take the institution into a new 'golden age' of rehabilitation. However, this too is a delusion:

[...] modernisation is a seductive and elusive concept which has been deployed to legitimate and support investment in the prison estate [...] the logic employed within the modernisation agenda since the 1950s – that 'new' or 'modern' prison places will considerably enhance safety levels, while offering prisoners 'the best chance to be rehabilitated and turn their lives around' [...] is simply a matter of unevidenced blind faith. Rather than a policy designed to enhance prison performance based on robust evidence and rigorous analysis, modernisation is a seductive and elusive strategy that has played a majorly significant role in securing support for new prison buildings and penal expansionism (Jones et al, 2024).

Reformism and modernisation are linked in one key respect. Both are fundamentally limited in that they must not *and* cannot support changes which are too radical or transformative because this would undermine the very existence of the prison and indeed the state itself. Although writing in a different context, Tom Nairn captured the chilling effect of this mentality on thinking about, and impelmenting, fundamental change: 'reform must not affect or weaken the instrument of reform: the State itself, the class or individual whose authority is being exercised. *Modernization must always stop short of self-liquidation'* (Nairn, 1988: 158, emphasis added).

Privatisation will defuse the crisis

It has been claimed that privatising prisons, and contracting out internal services, will provide the answer to defusing the crisis. This claim is also based on a number of myths and misconceptions.

The first private prison was opened in 1992. And yet, over 30 years on, privatisation has not become the dominant state strategy for organising and running prisons. The majority of people inside are still held in state-run prisons. Out of 122 prisons, only 14 are privately run. This is not to dismiss the detrimental impact of privatisation across *every* area of social life during this period, including prisons. Nor is it to underestimate the negative impact in contracting out services such as electronic monitoring and prison escorts. However, it *is* to say that the construction of the binary between public and private prisons distracts attention from the fact that the majority of people in prison still serve their sentences in state-run institutions. And whether the focus is on public or private institutions, they are *still* prisons. Furthermore, the questions that were asked in the late 1980s remain relevant today. Is it morally right that private, profit-driven interests are involved in punishing human beings? To whom are these institutions democratically accountable? Are private institutions any more efficient than state-run prisons? And do they result in cost savings? (Ryan and Ward, 1989).

There are other issues. The private company G4S was implicated in the death of Jimmy Mubenga. Jimmy was forcibly restrained by three security guards as he was being deported to Angola. After a convoluted legal process, the guards were found not guilty of manslaughter. However, it was subsequently revealed that one of them had written a racist text message telling deportees to:

Fuck off and go home you free-loading, benefit-grabbing, kid-producing, violent, non-English-speaking, cock suckers and take those hairy-faced, sandal-wearing, bomb-making, goat-fucking, smelly rag head bastards with you (cited in Blakeley, 2024: 118).

Additionally, 'hundreds of complaints' have been made over the years by people held in detention and deportation centres run by the company including racial abuse, choking, and unacceptable levels of force. It has also been accused of 'paying far under the minimum wage' to migrants who they used as prison labour and of 'using torture techniques – including electroshock therapy and forced injections – at its network of prisons in South Africa' (Blakeley, 2024: 118–119).

Private sector involvment has added an insidious, disastrous layer to other areas of the criminal injustice system as the botched privatisation of the probation service graphically illustrates. When he became the minister responsible for the service, Rory Steweart claimed 'it had all gone wrong' (Stewart, 2023: 296). The companies involved had failed to reduce reoffending rates which meant that they owed the government money. To cut costs, they made staff redundant and reduced their services:

> And because the contracts had been left deliberately unspecified, to encourage innovation, there was no way of forcing the companies even to meet offenders. The reoffending rate rose further. The companies owed the government tens of millions. At which point, instead of paying us, they were threatening to declare bankruptcy, abandoning tens of thousands of ex-offenders in the community. Abstract theorising and ill-considered ideology best left in a twenty-page report in a think tank, had blown up the system (Stewart, 2023: 296).

Privatising the probation service had devastating consequences. In June 2022, Jordan McSweeney attempted to rape and then murdered Zara Aleena. At this point, the service was split between private community rehabilitation companies who supervised low to medium-risk cases and the National Probation Service (NPS) who supervised high-risk cases. The 'profit-driven London Community Rehabilitation Company' was responsible for McSweeney's supervision. However, despite receiving reports about his violent behaviour and the 'serious risk he posed to women' he was still assessed as posing a medium-risk to them:

> With inaccurate risk assessment a key feature of the case, the [probation] inspectorate concluded that, had McSweeney been correctly assessed, the planning for the release, licence conditions and action taken by the NPS when he failed to turn up for appointments could have been considerably different. The funding arrangements for the private, profit-oriented companies provided a monetary incentive for employees not to assess cases as high-risk,

as this would result in them being passed on to the state-owned NPS, and a loss of income. Consequently, risk was routinely downgraded. If anyone has 'blood on their hands', it is the neoliberal ideologues in this government who, ignoring warnings issued in 2015 and 2016 by the inspectorate that resettlement arrangements were not fit for purpose, pursued this flawed and ultimately doomed experiment to its predictable tragic end (Hobbs, 2023).

The Prison Officers Association (POA) has also criticised the privatisation agenda. However, the POA's criticism is based on another myth. It implies that in the pre-privatised era prisons were well-functioning, benevolent institutions geared towards rehabilitating people inside. It is claimed that returning to this era will solve the crisis. The POA's claim ignores the alternative history outlined in Chapter 2 concerning the prison's abject failure to fulfil its official goals, including rehabilitation, *before* prison privatisation began in the early 1990s.

Privatisation is *not* the solution to the systemic crisis facing prisons and the wider criminal justice system. The binary distinction drawn between state-run and private institutions distracts attention from the desperately real issues facing both sets of institutions and the people held in them.

People in prison are rehabilitated inside

While there might have been the odd exception, regimes based on rehabilitation have never been an option for people in prison. Rather, for 200 years, punishment, security and control have dominated prison life. This has led to the degradation and dehumanisation of those inside while failing to cut reoffending rates. As the great American writer and activist James Baldwin observed in remarks that are wholly applicable to the treatment of people in prison: '[p]eople who treat other people as less than human must not be surprised when the bread they have cast on the waters comes floating back to them, poisoned' (Baldwin, 1972: 192).

In psychoanalytical terms, the state's goal has been to generate 'apathetic compliance' amongst prisoners (Khan cited in Phillips, 2021: 18). Beyond that, there is virtually nothing in terms of rehabilitation.

Even on their own terms, the state, and successive governments, have failed to provide the programmes necessary for the rehabilitation they wrongfully claim prisons are capable of delivering. For example, compared with 2010, there were nearly 12,000 fewer prisoners – a fall of 74% – involved in rehabilitation courses in 2023 (Syal, 2024a).

Additionally, the Prisons Inspectorate has pointed out that they have criticised the lack of purposeful activity inside for years. The Inspectorate uses a number of tests to capture the health, or otherwise of individual prisons. Purposeful activity has always been the lowest scoring of these tests. In 2022/23, it was 'worse than ever'. Of the prisons they inspected, only one men's prison was rated as 'good or reasonably good':

> The norm in most jails has become prisoners locked in their cells for many hours during the day or hanging round on wings with not enough to do. Ofsted reports that the standards of education in prison are very poor, attendance is appalling and there are not enough courses or work experience available to prepare prisoners for their eventual release. The idea that pushing a mop around a wing for an hour and then hanging round with nothing to do for the rest of the day is any sort of preparation for getting a job is fanciful, but for many prisoners this is as close as they get to anything approaching work (HM Inspectorate of Prisons, 2023a).

In February 2024, it was revealed that the Department of Education had missed its target 'by at least 90 per cent, after fewer than 10 people serving time in prison have started apprenticeships in England since long-awaited legislation was introduced in September 2022' (Patel, 2024). According to the Prisons Inspectorate, even an institution such as Rochester, which was specifically designed as a training and resettlement prison, was failing to rehabilitate people inside. Less than a third of them were engaged in purposeful activity. The provision of skills work and education was designated as inadequate which was the lowest assessment that could be given by Ofsted. The majority of prisoners 'had nothing to do' while the prison's wings were 'chaotic and poorly supervised'. Offender management was 'ineffective' and the arrangements for public protection were 'not fit for purpose'. The physical environment was hardly conductive to rehabilitation either:

> Most of the accommodation remained very dilapidated with some of the worst conditions we have seen in recent years. Both staff and prisoners told us that rats and mice regularly entered cells and offices on the older wings. Prisoners resorted to creating barriers from cardboard to fill gaps under cell doors to try and keep vermin out of their cells (HM Inspectorate of Prisons, 2024b).

Finally, to return to a point made in Chapter 2. The discourse of rehabilitation presupposes that people in prison are being released back to a society that is equal, welcoming and socially inclusive. However, the reverse is the case. They are returning to a grossly unequal society which negatively labels and socially excludes them. This raises profound questions about the *meaning* of rehabilitation, and its operationalisation, in such a society:

> What does it mean to rehabilitate a person to their former state if that state involves poverty, racism, unemployment, unstable housing, and/or violence? Can a person be rehabilitated if they have never been habilitated (or made fit or capable for society)? (Law, 2021: 26).

Prisons are democratically accountable

The claim that prisons are democratically accountable is the final myth and misrepresentation considered in this chapter. In practice, they are beyond democratic control. Their regimes have always been, and continue to be, based on a 'conscious disregard of justice' (Simmons cited in Halpert, 2024). There are a number of reasons for this.

First, prison staff are protected from scrutiny by an insidious culture of immunity and impunity. It is ironic that prisoners are often blamed for undermining justice by refusing to divulge details about crimes they, and others, may have committed. In other words, they should not 'grass'. However, what about the code of silence – the occupational omerta – that dominates staff culture, particularly when a serious event occurs such as a death in custody?

Second, in the eyes of prisoners, the complaints system is discredited. The Prisons and Probation Ombudsman (PPO) found that there was 'a considerable lack of trust in the whole [...] process' amongst the people in prison who participated in a PPO survey. They thought that:

> [...] it was harder for prisoners for whom English was not their first language to make a complaint [...] None of the staff interviewed could recall any prisoners asking to submit a complaint in a different language [...] Many participants said they had never had responses to their complaints. Staff also acknowledged that complaints were not always answered [...] When presented with a scenario in which racial discrimination was a potential issue, some participants stated it would be a waste of time submitting a complaint. A few then suggested that racism is too pervasive in the prison service to be able to act against it. Comments from staff indicated a lack of meaningful consideration of ethnicity (Reed, 2022: 4 and 6).

Third, there is the myth that those who manage and staff prisons learn lessons and implement recommendations so that previous errors and mistakes are not repeated. However, the system for enforcing and implementing recommendations, even those made by official bodies, is also discredited. Few recommendations are rarely, if ever, implemented. In evidence to the House of Commons Justice Committee, Peter Clarke, the former Chief Inspector of Prisons, said that '2018–19 was the third year running that fewer recommendations were achieved than not achieved' (cited in House of Commons Justice Committee, 2019: 65). He went on:

When you look at the five prisons [now six] that have so far been subjected to the urgent notification process, one of the common factors *is an utterly appalling response to recommendations in the past*. How that was allowed to happen for so long is still something of a mystery to me, but I hope that in the future transparency and accountability is seen as a strength, not a weakness, on the part of the Prison Service (House of Commons Justice Committee, 2019: 65–66, emphasis added).

More recent data from the Prisons Inspectorate confirms Peter Clarke's point. In 2022/3, the Inspectorate made 1619 recommendations. Of these, 639 (39%) were achieved, 177 (11%) were partially achieved and 803 (50%) were not achieved (HM Chief Inspector of Prisons for England and Wales, 2023: 108). When Lowdham Grange was inspected, of the 83 recommendations made in a previous inspection and scrutiny visit, 16 (19%) had been achieved, 4 (5%) had been partially achieved and 63 (76%) had *not* been achieved (HM Inspectorate of Prisons (2023b: 50–58).

Writing in 2023, Tom McNeill pointed out that, even when official bodies like the Prisons and Probation Ombudsman and coroners have 'found repeated, wide-ranging and significant failings by the Prison Service in the management of prisoners at risk of self-harm which have contributed to many [self-inflicted deaths]' little if anything was done because the prison service was shielded by the ancient (and scandalous) doctrine of Crown Immunity. In practice, this means that Crown bodies, including prisons, cannot be prosecuted for breaching their duties under the Health and Safety at Work Act. They can be '"censured" by the [Health and Safety Executive] – but this is merely a reprimand by an obscure non-statutory process that is not open to the public [...] The last reported "Crown Censure" taken by the HSE in relation to prison suicide was over 10 years ago' (McNeill, 2023). For some, however, prisons could be, and indeed should be prosecuted under the Corporate Manslaughter and Corporate Homicide Act 2007, not least where a series of failures of senior management over time lead to foreseeable deaths (Tombs, 2016b).

And even when coroners follow their statutory duty and issue Prevention of Future Deaths (PFD) reports which alert prisons, NHS trusts and other bodies, if they believe there is a 'risk that future deaths could occur unless action is taken' then 'recipients are obliged to respond in writing but *are not required to take concrete steps to address the concerns identified by coroners*' (O'Neill and Hayton, 2025, emphasis added). According to Georgia Richards, there were 82,000 preventable deaths recorded by the Office for National Statistics in 2022, in other words deaths which could have been avoided. And although there were over 5000 PFD reports issued between 2013 and January 2025:

> [...] it was impossible to know anything about what action that might or might not have been taken following a coroner's report [...] the system doesn't work, it's a waste of time. There are very few PFDs that have led to meaningful change and often it's not the PFD that triggered it. Change comes from additional factors like change in leadership of the organisation, huge media scrutiny or dedicated families (cited in O'Neill and Hayton, 2025).

Conclusion

The data in this chapter indicates that *even on their own terms*, prisons are a failure and that this failure is mystified by a number of myths and mis-representations. The following chapter considers the radical alternative to the centuries-long failure of the prison to fulfil its official goals. This radical alternative is built on the idea of abolishing prisons in their present form.

what should we do? The case for abolishing prisons

The previous chapters discussed the historical and contemporary failure of prisons to fulfil their official goals while generating physical and psychological harms which have dehumanised, diminished and degraded the people detained within them. So what should be done? The answer to this question lies in developing an 'abolitionist imagination' and, through this, abolishing prisons in England and Wales (Scott, 2020a: 207).

Misrepresenting abolitionists

Before considering the theoretical and practical basis of abolitionism, it is important to recognise that abolitionists are consistently demonised. They are constructed as utopian, out-of-touch, starry-eyed extremists who, unlike state agents and liberal academics, lack objectivity and whose policies are impossible to put into practice. Through this, the state consistently attempts to 'define [them] out' of the debate about prisons (Mathiesen, 1980: 288–289). It is also claimed – wrongly – that they wish to free *every* prisoner irrespective of their offence. This derogatory 'truth' – unscrupulously peddled by an insidious, hypocritical network of state agents, politicians and media commentators – is designed to discredit abolitionism. In turn, it justifies the condescending dismissal of abolitionists *without* actually engaging with their ideas, while defending policies which have failed drastically for centuries.

Abolitionists are also offensively defamed for being pro-crime and anti-victim. In fact, the reverse is the case. By ignoring the social harms arising from the rampant criminality of the powerful, it is this network which has been pro-crime. The systemic indifference to male violence against women and girls, and to racist, homophobic and transphobic violence, illustrates the cynical depth of their hypocrisy regarding victims and survivors. This network *does* support victims and survivors but only those, and their relatives, who demand vengeance and retribution. Those who articulate empathic compassion, even when terrible crimes have been commit-ted against them, or against a family member, are systematically ignored (Scott and Sim, 2023: 13).

In 2020, two abolitionists, engaged as expert witnesses in a case involving the proposed release of a terminally ill prisoner, experienced this negative stereotyping. Arguing against the prisoner's release, the govern-ment's legal team was led by Sir James Eadie KC. According to his law firm's website, Eadie was the 'simply phenomenal [...] towering giant [...] mind-blowingly good... go-to silk for the UK government'. His team's court submission argued that the prisoner relied on:

> [...] concerns expressed by Dr Scott and Professor Sims [sic] in their report prepared on 12 April 2020 in support of this claim [...] They are criminologists, with a history of research and publications *arguing against imprisoning offenders* (Skeleton Argument of the Secretary of State, 2020: Paragraph 77, emphasis added).

Rather than engaging with the extensive evidence which had been mar-shalled and the decades-long research records of both academics, the government's lawyers mobilised the age-old, offensive stereotype that, as abolitionists, they were automatically against 'imprisoning offenders'.

The ominous lack of engagement with, and ongoing silencing of, abo-litionism was also evident in a Parliamentary Briefing Paper on prison population growth published in January 2024. The paper contained 32 pages and 173 references and was designed to '*support Members of Parliament*' (Jones and Lally, 2024: 2, emphasis added). There were no references to the literature, research and policy proposals painstakingly developed by abolitionists for decades. Instead, the paper pointed to literature, research and policies which had been endlessly repeated over the same period. The paper's uncritical message to those at the centre of formulating penal policy was that reform, not fundamental transformation, was still the way forward for a system convulsed by yet another deep and damaging crisis.

Abolitionism: Morality, language and action

Abolitionism is an interlocking political *and* moral movement (Scott, 2018; Scott 2020a). This includes consistently highlighting the state's dissembling and deceit around prisons and the criminal injustice system more generally. Abolitionists not only speak truth *to* power but also demand truth *from* power (Sim, 2023b). They insist that it is morally imperative to humanise people in prison – and those held in police cells, psychiatric hospitals, immigration removal centres, youth justice institutions and other state-run and private sites of detention – through recognising their everyday, dehumanising experiences and to listen to their voices which have 'been buried and... disqualified' (Foucault, 2003: 8). This includes describing those inside as people in prison rather than using the label 'prisoners' as the 'application of the label... is predicated on the construction of a negative, dehumanised, one-dimensional caricature of the offender situated solely in the nature of their "crime"' (Scott, 2008: 184). Doing so challenges their state-induced estrangement and alienation from the wider society, as well as undermining the dominant, popular and political narrative which constructs them as less eligible, duplicitous 'animals' who deserve to be punished. Adopting an abolitionist morality also means humanising their families who are stigmatised and labelled by the state, politicians and the media as 'disorganised', 'chaotic' and 'feral' and who are seen as somehow being 'responsible' for their relatives' behaviour. This, in itself, is both ironic and hypocritical, given that the social harms which have the most searing impact on peoples' lives are generated, overwhelmingly, by those who come from stable, orderly, 'respectable', backgrounds, a point which is almost universally ignored in the debates about law, order and prisons.

Abolitionism rejects the reformism discussed in Chapter 2. And while abolitionists recognise that there have been *some* reforms at *some* points which have made a material difference to *some* prisoners 'frameworks that rely exclusively on reforms help to produce the stultifying idea that nothing lies beyond the prison' (Davis, 2003: 20). To move 'beyond the prison', they demand policies which will radically transform the institution *and* the wider social conditions which 'allow harm and violence to flourish' (Law, 2021: 178). They refuse to use the state's language which constructs a particular 'truth' about prisons and the people held in them: '[t]he more we use the language of the powerful, the more attuned we become to defining the problems at hand as *the powerful usually do*; in other words, the more integrated we become into the old system' (Mathiesen, 1974: 19, original emphasis). Following Mathiesen, abolitionists advocate pursuing 'non-reformist reforms' 'which work to undermine or shrink a harmful system [in this case the prison] rather than strengthening or normalising it' (Lamble, 2022). Furthermore:

> [w]hile non-reformist reforms will not, in and of themselves, abolish prisons – that requires broader social, political and economic change – these strategies help avoid the trap of conventional reforms, moving towards changes that reduce the size, scope and power of prisons (Lamble, 2022).

Abolitionists maintain that their strategies for radical change are not unrealistic, idealistic or extremist and that the existence of prisons is *not* inevitable. The institution's presence should not induce hopelessness and helplessness because 'there are always cracks, contradictions and therefore opportunities' in this case for radical penal transformation (Hall et al, 2013: 20). This struggle is difficult particularly in the context of an increasingly authoritarian state and a mass media and social media complex which, despite the 'cracks and contradictions' within and between them, will defend the existing status quo – penal and social – whatever the human cost.

Abolitionists advocate replacing the non-action, top-down strategy of reformism, so ingrained in the praxis of state agents and liberal reform groups, in favour of pursuing a radical strategy of direct action from below involving critical academics, activists, grassroots organisations, charities, people in prison, those who have been released from prison and the families of people who have died in prison and in other state and privately run institutions. This strategy has involved the occupation of the Visitor's Centre in Holloway by Sisters Uncut in May 2017 who pointed out that, '[p]risons are an inhumane response to social problems faced by vulnerable women – the government should provide a better answer' (cited in Sim, 2023a: 904). Abolitionists have also become company shareholders to contest 'state-corporate power.' This has included members of the Reclaim Justice Network protesting at the Annual General Meetings of G4S which forced the company to withdraw 'from its controversial delivery of child detention in Israel' (Scott, 2020a: 179). Like other grassroots organisations, they reject '[...] the myths that prisons, surveillance and policing can solve social and economic problems. We seek alternatives that keep our communities safe and achieve real social justice' (Community Action on Prison Expansion, cited in Sim, 2023a: 904).

Imagining a prison-free future

How can penal power be contested and how can a prison-free future be achieved? For abolitionists, the answer to this question lies in pursuing and implementing radical policies for fundamental, transformative change. The chapter now considers a number of these policies.

Stop building prisons and close existing institutions

Halting the prison building programme, and reducing the number of prisons, is a key abolitionist demand. As Chapter 4 noted, in 1983, the biggest prison building programme of the twentieth century was announced. Forty years on, it has failed to alleviate the crisis. More prisons mean more people being sentenced by the courts to serve more time so the vicious, debilitating cycle of crisis/reform/crisis/reform is endlessly repeated. The misleading claim that building new prisons will alleviate the appalling conditions inside is a distraction from the key issue: too many people are sent to prison *irrespective* of the conditions. Dartmoor was opened in 1809, and was soon crowded. In 1979, the May Inquiry recommended that the prison should be closed yet it remains operational, despite the major prison building programmes which have been carried out since then. Over 40 years after the inquiry reported, the prison still had problems including prisoners who were:

> […] subjected to cramped conditions, with inadequate amounts of furniture, for long periods of the day. Leaders had partially screened off in-cell toilets, but prisoners were still in full view of their cellmate while using them. To alleviate this issue, some prisoners had made a screen from a prison bed sheet, risking being placed on report and a potential sanction (HM Inspectorate of Prisons, 2023c: 21).

Stopping the building programme runs parallel with the abolitionist demand to close existing institutions. Again, this is not based on unrealistic idealism. In fact, in July 2024, the Justice Secretary announced that Dartmoor would be *temporarily* closed. And, despite the political hostility to fully closing prisons, there *is* a historical precedent for this. Between 1908 and 1939, 'about 20 prisons were closed, despite the crime rate in this period actually increasing by around 160 per cent' (Wilson, cited in Bhui, 2024: 76).

Develop radical alternatives to prison

Abolitionists argue that it is pointless introducing alternatives to prison unless the building programme is stopped. Building more and bigger prisons will only result in alternatives being absorbed into the system while the prison population will continue to grow. Therefore, what is needed are *radical* alternatives to prisons. For the abolitionist Ruth Wilson Gilmore, 'the prison abolition movement is not just about abolishing unjust institutions, but about building just alternatives' (cited in Ransby, 2015). To do this, abolitionists reject:

> [...] prisonlike substitutes for the prison, such as house arrest, safeguarded by electronic surveillance bracelets. Rather, positing decarceration as our overarching strategy, we would try to envision a continuum of alternatives to imprisonment – demilitarization of schools, revitalisation of education at all levels, a health system that provides free physical and mental care to all and a justice system based on reparation and reconciliation rather than retribution and vengeance [...] alternatives that fail to address racism, male dominance, homophobia, class bias, and other forms of domination will not, in the final analysis, lead to decarceration and will not advance the goal of abolition (Davis, 2003: 107–108).

Demanding radical alternatives is entirely distinct from the reformist logic which has prevailed for so long. In articulating this demand, abolitionists have been accused of being unrealistic. Not so. For decades, they *have* clearly identified realistic and radical alternatives to the policies, both inside and outside, which have dismally failed for centuries. Outside prisons, they have supported programmes for men accused of domestic violence. They have recognised both the horrendous nature of this violence *and* the problem of incarcerating the few violent men who are convicted in a hyper-masculine institution like the prison. And while not without their own issues including 'inadequate facilities and resources' (Morran, 2022), these programmes, based on feminist praxis, have challenged the pivotal role of 'gender, power and domination' intrinsic to male violence and changed the perpetrators' violent behaviour (Dobash et al, cited in Sim, 2023a: 902). However, 'despite their positive impact', the programmes 'remain, at best, marginal, and, at worst, ignored by the state which continues to rely on tried, tested and failed law and order responses' to male violence. Abolitionist feminists would argue that these responses reinforce the 'individualistic discourse of male violence through concentrating on the dangerous predator while distracting attention from the systemic and widespread nature of this violence' (Sim, 2023a: 902).

In terms of prisons, Pat Carlen has outlined a radical, realistic pro-gramme of action, arguing that women's prisons should be abolished for an experimental period of five years, while 100 places would be retained for women accused of serious crimes:

> To reduce the prison population we must first reduce the number of prisons; to reduce the number of prisons we must first abolish certain categories of imprisonment. Women's imprisonment is, for several reasons, a prime candidate for abolition [...] The choice is between continuing to squander millions of pounds on prisons or taking bold steps to stop legislators and sentencers seeing the prisons as being the ultimate panacea for all political, social and penal ills (Carlen, 1990: 121 and 125).

And, contrary to the myth that they have no practical suggestions for insti-tuting change short of simply abolishing prisons, there *are* alternatives which abolitionists have supported. Although it was based in Scotland, the Barlinnie Special Unit has been recognised in England and Wales, and internationally, as the most important innovation in British prisons in the last five decades. The Unit illustrated the pivotal role that prison regimes and the staff working in them *can* play in changing the attitudes and behaviour of people in prison, *not* through violence and dehumanisation but with empathy, compassion and understanding. The Unit held those pejoratively labelled as Scotland's most violent prisoners – the 'animals'. And yet assaults on staff were non-existent. The Unit would not have suc-ceeded without the staff, a point recognised by the prisoners themselves (Boyle, 1984). Ken Murray, its Principal Officer, described its philosophy in words which still resonate today and from which the state, the media and liberal reform groups could learn:

[...] the methods that we introduced into the... Unit... are based on a very simple attitude, that being that we should speak to the prisoners and suggest to them that we should, together find ways and means best suited for the method where we could live tolerably with each other... *There's never been one single incident of a prison officer being attacked in the Special Unit by a prisoner* (cited in Sim, 2008: 187, emphasis added).

The regime in the Special Unit, and in other institutions such as Parkhurst C Wing and Grendon Underwood, have clearly illustrated that people in prison can fundamentally change if they experience an environment built on individual responsibility *and* institutional accountability and which is non-judgmental, non-retributive and supportive (Sim, 2009). Their praxis make these regimes dangerous *not* because of the people they detain but because they illustrate the traditional system's abject failure to change those inside. They have *never* been welcomed by politicians, the state and the media because they challenge their often-pathological emphasis on punishment and retribution as the *only* answer to crime. The Special Unit and C Wing are no longer operational while the principles underpinning Grendon's regime have never been significantly extended since the prison opened in 1962, *over* 60 years ago. It is a shameful indictment of the road travelled by penal policy for decades. These regimes have been small islands in a sea of punishment and retribution.

There are other, contemporary examples of non-retributive regimes whose operations stand in marked contrast to the dominant discourses of punishment and retribution. They include Warren Hill, described as:

[...] the safest category C prison in the country, having the lowest levels of self-harm and violence among comparable establishments. It was a thoroughly respectful place, with strong staff-prisoner relationships being a defining feature. The accommodation was fit for purpose, there was excellent time out of cell and the range of activities, both educational and extra-curricular, was impressive (HM Inspectorate of Prisons, 2020: 7).

To be clear, this is *not* an argument for reforming prisons rather than abolishing them. These places are a *stepping stone* for the radical, transformative change that is required. However, it *is* pointing out that even when alternatives within the existing system have worked, they have been marginalised, denigrated, ignored or closed because of the dangers they pose to the traditional system.

Redirect state spending

As Chapter 4 indicated, despite the cuts, expenditure on prisons and on the criminal justice system more generally remains huge. Over £14.6 billion was spent on various Ministry of Justice (MoJ) 'services' in 2023–24, including over £6.5 billion on prisons and probation (National Audit Office, 2024a: 10). At the end of October 2024, the funding for new prisons was confirmed: £2.3 billion was to be spent over the next two years, a further £500 million on recruiting prison and probation staff, and over £500 million on prison and probation service maintenance. Funding for prosecutions was to rise to over £1 billion in 2025/26, a real terms increase of 7.5%. In contrast, investment in services such as access to legal aid was not mentioned (Rogerson, 2024). Spending on legal aid had fallen by over £700 million between 2012–13 and 2022–23. According to the National Audit Office, the MoJ had introduced reforms in 2013 '*to discourage unnecessary litigation and make significant savings*' (National Audit Office, 2024a: 15, emphasis added). Not surprisingly, the Ministry had failed both in social justice terms with respect to the access defendants had to funding but also in relation to the sanctified, neoliberal goal of achieving value for money:

> [...] more than a decade on, MoJ still lacks an understanding of the full costs and benefits of its reforms. Our findings concluded that [the] MoJ does not know whether everyone eligible for legal aid can access it and that the government needs to do more to ensure the sustainability of the legal aid market if it is to achieve value for money (National Audit Office, 2024a: 15).

The cost of the building programme was already spiralling. The government's target of 20,000 new places was unlikely to be reached until 2031, five years later than planned, and was expected to be at least £4.2 billion, or 80% more than the original estimate (National Audit Office, 2024b). That is a scandal in itself. No doubt the money would be found, legitimated by Shabana Mahmood, the Labour government's Justice Secretary's claim that 'we will always treat prisons as of "national importance"' (Gov.UK. 2024a). As ever, those providing social and welfare services would continue to struggle for funding. Compared with prisons, the government, like its predecessors, did not regard policies in these areas to be of 'national importance'.

While law and order 'services' were still generously funded, despite the cuts, grassroots organisations and charities were operating, as ever, in a 'state of continuous scarcity' (Levine and Meiners, 2020: 27). Even services close to the heart of successive governments like Victim Support were to be cut by 4.2% in 2025 while the Rape and Sexual Abuse Support Fund was to remain at £21 million and would not be increased in line with inflation. At the same time, the budget for the Ministry of Justice was to increase by 4.3% in real terms (Lawrie, 2024). And even when funding was available, the money was not being spent. According to the National Audit Office, in the context of what was widely regarded as an 'epidemic of violence against women and girls [VAWG]', which was 'getting worse', the Home Office 'did not have "centrally coordinated funding" for VAWG, unlike that for the 2021 illegal drugs strategy, and had underspent on its own VAWG budget by an average of 15% between 2021–22 and 2023–24' (cited in Topping, 2025).

Funding for organisations not close to the government was even more precarious. In August 2024, Rape Crisis England and Wales announced that it would reduce its services due to issues with their core funding:

The anticipated reduction of services and loss of Rape Crisis centres comes at a time when demand continues to increase; last year alone, Rape Crisis centres supported over 80,000 victims and survivors of sexual violence and abuse, a quarter of whom were children. This year, centres are already oversubscribed – nearly 14,000 survivors are waiting for a service, and the latest analysis of Rape Crisis waiting list data revealed that over 80% of those on waiting lists were waiting for specialist counselling services (Rape Crisis England and Wales, 2024).

Fifty women's centres, which ensured that vulnerable women were diverted from prison, were predicted to reach a funding 'cliff edge' by the end of March 2025 due to a gap of at least £5.1 million in their finances (Khan, cited in Osuh, 2024). The gap constituted 0.035% of the MoJ's budget for 2023–24 and 0.12% of the extra £4.2 billion needed for the prison building programme which, as noted above, the government is unlikely to have a problem in finding. It is also worth noting that it was £175 million less than the £180 million claimed by MPs and Peers in expenses between August 2019 and July 2022 which included claims for 'business class flights, hotels, iPads and professional photoshoots' (Williams, 2023).

Abolitionists would argue that the traditional funding model has delivered little, if anything by way of the prison's official goals, never mind delivering social justice. It is a lottery. State institutions receive funding *as a matter of course* while grassroots organisations and charities struggle to survive on a daily basis, despite the enormous contribution they make to the wider social good. Therefore, state funding should be radically transformed. It should be redirected away from criminal justice responses to conventional crime which, even on their own terms, have miserably failed. Instead, there should be investment in welfare-orientated, radical alternatives to prison including: physical and mental health care services which respond to the specific needs of different groups; social care; social and inexpensive housing; education; youth clubs; drug support networks; environmental protection; health and safety at work; child support; nursery and play group provision; children's services; rape crisis centres and miscarriage of justice organisations. In other words, 'creating a world where people's needs are met' (Law, 2021: 154).

Abolish punitive sentencing

Abolitionists challenge the myth that long, retributive sentences are effective in deterring individuals from conventional crime, never mind deterring those in positions of power. As Chapter 3 noted, the number of people serving life and indeterminate sentences in England and Wales has been rising exponentially.

Do these numbers mean that dangerous behaviour is increasing? Or are sentences becoming longer and harsher? According to the Ministry of Justice, '[m]ore than two and a half times as many people were sentenced to 10 years or more in 2022 than in 2010' (Ministry of Justice, cited in Prison Reform Trust, 2024: 16). For abolitionists, these figures reflect an increase in punitive sentencing rather than an exponential growth in conventionally defined dangerous behaviour.

Has this pattern of sentencing made women and girls, for example, any safer? The answer is no. In fact, the link between reducing dangerousness and punitive sentencing is flimsy. Rather, the abject failure of prisons to guarantee safety, security and protection has led abolitionists to ask different questions which move beyond the state's narrow and self-defeating definition of these terms:

> How can we organise our communities to be safe? What should we do when various kinds of harm, with different kinds of needs, occur? What are the collective ways and forums in which we can pursue this work? (Brown and Schept, cited in Sim, 2023a: 901).

Punitive sentencing is based on another myth. Politicians who demand harsher punishments and longer sentences ignore the evidence that not *all* people at *all* times are inherently retributive, even in the most traumatic of circumstances. Gee Walker, whose son Anthony was brutally murdered in a racist attack on Merseyside, did not demand vengeance for her son's racist killers (Sim, 2009). In America, the relatives of people who have been murdered but who have not supported the death penalty for their killers illustrates what it means not just to be a human being but to be a *humane* human being. In spite of the ocean of grief into which individuals are plunged when they lose a relative to murder, they have promoted compassion and forgiveness rather than punishment and retribution. This is an issue which politicians *never* address in their unprincipled, vote-seeking drive for longer sentences, which, as noted above, even on their own terms, fail to deliver safety, security and protection.

Dismantle the occupational culture of prison staff

What should be done about the formal and informal authoritarian, occupational culture of prison staff which, despite some honourable exceptions, impacts so negatively on the lives of people in prison? This culture makes prisoners 'ghosts in the penal machine' through a range of techniques including denying the suffering they experience and their full humanity as human beings (Scott, 2008: 168). In raising this issue, abolitionists, once again, have been stereotyped and misrepresented. They are accused of painting all prison staff with the same Neanderthal brush. Not so. On the contrary, they recognise that there are some staff, in some institutions, who are committed to treating people in prison with dignity and respect but who themselves have been denigrated as 'care bears' by other staff because of their positive commitment to those inside (Sim, 2009).

Abolitionists are also accused of failing to offer policy solutions about the occupational culture. Again, not so. In terms of the violence by staff, discussed in Chapter 4, '[t]here are a number of things that *can be done* almost immediately to make the problem more visible' (Scott, 2020b, original emphasis). These include:

1. **Taking the issue seriously**: This would involve the development of a culture of 'zero tolerance' for all forms of violence and mechanisms put in place for the safe reporting and recording of prison officer violence and their appropriate investigation.

2. **Challenging the normalisation of physical violence in existing prison officer occupational culture**: This would include further training for prison officers in conflict resolution and non-violent forms of intervention; and awareness of mental health.
3. **Understanding the inherent antagonism of prison work**: This would mean locating prison work within [the] wider context of coercion, repression and domination and the use of physical violence in [the] last instance to maintain control.
4. **Recognition of the shared humanity of prisoners**: This would entail recognition of the harms, suffering, injury and violence of imprisonment; the indignity of prison for human beings; the pains and frustrations generated by prison on an everyday basis; and hearing the voice of the prisoner (Scott, 2020b, original emphasis).

What about staff training? Presently, at nine weeks, it is 'one of the shortest in Western Europe' (Acheson, 2024: 82). Previous accounts have painted a bleak picture of the experiences of new recruits:

> [...] a female officer commented that 'at training college you're taught never to trust the bastards' [...] Numerous new officers were shocked at the degree of verbal and psychological abuse meted out by their trainers [...] They claimed that corporate promotions of 'excellence', 'caring', 'quality' and 'respect' – terms that they had heard a great deal during their initial interviews – were barely evident in the organisational realities that they had experienced during this element of their basic training [...] Many of my interviewees, male and female, remarked upon the militaristic, paternalistic and abusive nature of their basic training (Crawley, cited in Sim, 2009: 147).

'Games' such as 'shag-tag' involved trainee officers bending over and touching their knees so that they could 'only be "released" by three thrusts (indicating sexual intercourse from the rear) from another officer (again male or female)' (Crawley, cited in Sim, 2009: 147).

What is the alternative? The curriculum and training recruits receive should be fundamentally transformed. In the context of a radically reduced prison population, supported by a network of radical alternatives to prison, training should be centred on civil liberties, human rights, social justice, psychotherapy and social welfare operationalised within an environment devoid of the nefarious and harmful impact of hegemonic masculinity whose destructive presence is so dominant in male prisons, in particular.

Democratising prisons and abolitionism

There is an 'accountability void' in prisons (Coles and Shaw, no date: 25). As Chapter 4 illustrated, the abject and unjustifiable failure to implement recommendations from the Prisons Inspectorate, the Prisons and Probation Ombudsman and coroners graphically illustrates the magnitude of this void.

In essence, the harms generated by prison regimes, and their often devastating impact on people inside, continue unabated. For abolitionists, as an *initial* first step, prisons need to be made democratically accountable so that staff at all levels, from managers to those working on the wings and landings, are accountable for their everyday actions *and* non-actions. Controlling the discretionary exercise of penal power, abolishing the institutionalised culture of immunity and impunity, dismantling the formal and informal authoritarian, occupational staff culture, making state institutions responsible for what happens inside and demanding 'truth, justice and accountability' – the slogan around which the charity INQUEST campaigns in relation to preventable deaths inside and outside of prisons – would be *stepping stones* in the drive towards abolishing prisons. Embedding structures of democratic accountability would not be restricted to prisons but would be applied to the whole system so that 'criminal justice personnel [w]ould be accountable not only for *who* they criminalise, but *why*, and in *whose* interests' (Box, 1983: 223, original emphasis).

Democratising prisons, the criminal in justice system and the state more generally, is the beginning *not* the end of the process for their radical transformation and eventual abolition. Karl Marx recognised this. For him, the complete 'democratization of society' was dependent on, and reflected in, the 'democratization in the state' (Draper, cited in Panitch and Albo, 2017: xiv). In other words, 'we need a definition of democracy that makes determinate demands on institutions; that we can use to criticise institutions like capitalism and the state and use to guide their process of replacement' (Raekstad, 2017: 271).

In terms of deaths in prison, the failure to learn lessons, discussed in Chapter 4, is particularly acute. The charity INQUEST has consistently highlighted the dire implications arising from the state's failure to implement recommendations from coroners and independent inquiries:

> [...] the public and bereaved families need transparency, accountability and action, so that changes are made to protect us and our families and prevent future deaths. Hundreds of vital recommendations are made following inquests and inquiries. Yet there is no system in place to oversee them or ensure changes are made. Potentially life-saving recommendations are too often forgotten, dismissed or simply not implemented. This leads to yet more preventable deaths and harms (INQUEST, no date, original emphasis).

In order to develop a system based on transparency and accountability, the charity has called for a radical policy overhaul involving establishing a National Oversight Mechanism. This would be a 'new independent public body responsible for collating, analysing and following-up on recommendations arising from inquests, inquiries, official reviews and investigations into state-related deaths' (INQUEST, no date).

Abolitionism and social justice

Despite the state's claim to the contrary, delivering justice has *never* been a priority for its institutions. In terms of prisons, although written in 1993, Barbara Hudson's point is entirely relevant over thirty years on, perhaps even more so: 'penal policy [...] does not seem to be achieving even criminal justice, still less contributing to social justice' (Hudson, 1993: 148).

The abysmal treatment of the victims and survivors of male violence against women and girls graphically and poignantly illustrates this point. So too does the non-prosecution of domestic violence cases. In the year to March 2024, there were over 850,000 recorded cases of 'domestic abuse', which disproportionately impacted on women and girls, involving an estimated 2.3 million incidents. Just over 51,000 – 6% – resulted in a prosecution (Office for National Statistics, 2024b). The state's systemic complacency and sheer indifference is also evident in its lamentable response to the victims and survivors of disasters and miscarriages of justice which, for decades, have devastated the lives of tens of thousands of people, leaving them scarred, bereft and traumatised.

For abolitionists, criminal injustice is the norm. This can be seen in the (non) response of the state, and successive governments, to the social harms generated by the criminality of the powerful. It is utterly compromised to the point of being virtually non-existent. If social justice is to be delivered then responding to the crimes committed by those with enormous economic, political and social power is fundamental. As a starting point, this would involve '[..]both resisting some efforts to criminalize conventional crimes, while promoting some efforts to criminalize economic crimes' (Alvesalo and Tombs, cited in Scott and Sim, 2023: 36). This is no easy task, as the impact, or rather the non-impact of the Corporate Manslaughter and Corporate Homicide Act 2007 indicates. Although it became law in 2008, by June 2024, only 32 convictions had been achieved under the Act (Holden, cited in Tombs, forthcoming). In other words, as Tombs points out, there were, on average, two prosecutions a year: '[t]o put this average... into context, most recent Health and Safety Executive data, for 2022/23, reveals in excess of 13,000 work-related deaths for one year alone (National Statistics, cited in Tombs, forthcoming). As with all of the figures concerning work-related deaths, this figure was 'itself certainly an under-estimate...'(Hämäläinen et al, cited in Tombs, forthcoming).

Those who exercise such power are also shielded by another deeply entrenched culture of immunity and impunity which reinforces the hypocritical, one-sided nature of law enforcement and the widespread social injustices that follow. The fact that HM Revenue and Customs had not brought charges against a single company six years after the Criminal Finances Act 2017 came into force – an act which was described as 'landmark legislation' for clamping down on corporate tax evasion – provides another potent reminder, among many, about what behaviour is criminalised and what behaviour remains in the shadows outside the reach *and* concerns of the state (Siddons, 2024). The system is ideologically and institutionally driven *not* to respond to the systemic, social harms perpetrated by the powerful and the wounding levels of trauma and victimisation these harms generate.

This issue remains as relevant as ever. Steve Tombs has pointed out that nearly two and a half years after the Grenfell Tower fire in June 2017 which cost 72 lives, there had been '22 successful prosecutions involving 21 separate defendants'. The majority were prosecuted for low-level fraud. Furtheremore, 'most of those convicted fit a pattern: they are poor, marginalised individuals, overwhelmingly non-white... They are also often referred to in the media as "unemployed", "squatters", "homeless", and, most pejoratively of all, as "illegal immigrants"'. One case involved defrauding funds which were collected for the victims:

So [...] while defrauding funds collected for Grenfell victims might appear to be particularly deplorable, and none of this is to excuse this fraud, there is hardly a moral equivalence between the dispossessed – those consistently at the sharp end of state violence and coercion – seeking to secure somewhere to live or cash for food when compared with the life and death decision made by the richest council in England seeking to make what for them was a tiny saving in switching from less to more flammable cladding. These points made, the rapidity and punitiveness with which the criminal justice system has targeted marginalised offenders in the wake of the atrocity also provide a crucial context for understanding why the fire happened where and when it did in the first place (Tombs, 2019).

Similarly, by mid-July 2023, more than 28,000 people had been punished for often minor breaches of the rules governing COVID (McClenaghan, 2023). In contrast, up to June 2024, £7.3 billion of 'public money [had been] stolen by those abusing COVID schemes, according to the National Audit Office' (cited in *Private Eye*, 2024b: 14). At the time of writing, there is little sign that those stealing such vast sums will be held to account in the near future. Compare the glacial rate of progress involved in investigating and prosecuting these crimes with the state's lightning speed, and the undermining of due process, in the prosecution and punishment of the poor and vulnerable discussed in Chapter 3.

There is another hypocritical discourse at work here. The criminalisation and punishment of the poor and the powerless has been built on the highly contentious and misinformed political claim that the public want 'tougher punishments for criminals'. Even if this claim was true, then this begs another question: why have politicians not followed the logic of their own argument and recognised the public's demand for harsher punishments for the criminality of the powerful? (Fousiani and van Prooijen, 2023). The answer is clear. The state's hypocritical praxis continues to focus downward towards the politically and economically marginalised. Looking upwards at the criminality of the powerful, and responding to this criminality, has rarely, if ever, been integral to how state agents think and work, or how they are trained to think and work.

Implementing and sustaining a system based on social justice also means addressing another moral and political point concerning the choices available, or not available, to people in a deeply unequal society. Following Steven Box, Pat Carlen explored this issue through discussing the link between women, crime and poverty:

> [...] *although people choose to act, sometimes criminally, they do not do so under conditions of their own choosing.* Their choice makes them responsible, but the conditions make the choice comprehensible. These conditions, social and economic, contribute to crime because they constrain, limit or narrow the

choices available. Many of us, in similar circumstances, might choose the same course of action (Box, cited in Carlen, 1988: 162, original emphasis).

This point is important because it illustrates how poverty, destitution and systemic inequality curtail and restrict the choices people make. As Box and Carlen suggest, if people in the wider society discarded the cloak of hypocrisy then many in the same circumstances might make the same choice.

At the same time, as this book has shown, the most socially harmful and destructive acts are committed by individuals who are *not* poor. They engage in these acts in circumstances of their *own* choosing. However, unlike the poor and the vulnerable, their actions, in the majority of cases, are *not* targeted and criminalised by the state. A number of questions arise from this. What about their culpability for the devastation and destruction their actions cause? How can they be responsibilised? What about agency and intentionality? What role, if any, should the law play in holding them to account? These same questions can be asked about male violence. The sheer ubiquity of this violence, again which this book has shown, indicates that it is *not* confined solely to those caught in the pliers of poverty, or to those who hold economic and political power. It intersects with class and racial divisions and is deeply entwined with the politics of masculinity, and the exercise of patriarchal power.

If a socially just society is to materialise then these questions need to be addressed and acted upon. As yet, in the main, state institutions, politicians, the media and the wider society remain deeply unwilling to consider them and to face up to the radical policy implications which flow from answering them.

Abolish structural inequalities

Finally, as Chapter 2 illustrated, for 200 years the prison population has been drawn from the least powerful, and most vulnerable, groups in a society which is structurally and systemically unequal. The intersection between the social divisions of class, gender, 'race' sexuality, age and ability/disability, and the compassionless, capricious and coercive exercise of state power used to criminalise those at the bottom of this hierarchy of power, has generated a prison population that inevitably reflects these social divisions and structures of social inequality. For abolitionists, the radical transformation in prisons is directly linked to the abolition of these wider structures of power and powerlessness. This involves establishing a social system which embeds social justice for all rather than criminal injustice for the few. In the end, maximising social welfare, compassion and hope and minimising pain, retribution and despair are the foundation stones for building a world without prisons within a radically transformed social system.

6

conclusion

By 2024, it was clear that the prison system was not only in crisis but that it was unstable. Order inside was fractured and susceptible to collective and individual acts of contestation and insurrection. Recent disturbances in Bedford, Lewes, Swaleside, Birmingham, Winchester, Long Lartin, Featherstone, Erlestone and HMP Mount illustrated this point (Acheson, 2024). In June, specialist staff who were trained to respond to disturbances were called to Parc prison, a private prison run by G4S. This was a prison which had experienced ten deaths in three months and 17 altogether in the calendar year up to early December 2024 (Long, 2024; UK Parliament Committees, 2024). Additionally, in the 12 months to March 2024, there were other protests, including: 'incidents at height (7,783), followed by barricades or prevented access (1,827 incidents), concerted indiscipline (289 incidents) and hostages (58 incidents). All types of incidents of protesting behaviour increased [during this period] in comparison to the previous 12 months' (Ministry of Justice, 2024h).

These protests and incidents had different origins, motivations and meanings for those involved. Nonetheless, as the disturbance at Strangeways in 1990 illustrated – and in over 30 other prisons – if the grievances of people in prison are not addressed then something serious, widespread and damaging can occur resulting in loss of life. Protests and confrontations might not be immediate and are not inevitable but they have happened throughout prison history with the dire, human consequences which have often followed. And yet, despite the severity of the crisis in 2023 and 2024, including the disorder and confrontations referred to above, the idea of the prison remained so deeply entrenched and normalised that it continued to colonise political and popular consciousness. Like Mount Everest, it is regarded as a 'natural' phenomenon.

At the same time, despite everything, the institution continued to be the subject of puerile, political point scoring as politicians pursued short-term, expedient reforms to the detriment of the long-term structural change which was so desperately needed both inside and outside. This was particularly evident in the debates between the Conservative and Labour parties in the run up to, and beyond, the General Election in July 2024. When still in power, and in response to the crisis of capacity, the Conservatives announced an early release scheme. With depressing pre-dictability, Shabana Mahmood, Labour's then Shadow Secretary of State for Justice, was quick to make political capital from it:

It beggars belief that police are being told to sit on their hands and ignore crime because the Conservatives have mismanaged the criminal justice system so badly [...] *Labour is the party of law and order. We will build the new prisons needed and make Britain's streets safe* (cited in Dodd, 2024, emphasis added).

Mahmood's intervention was ironic given that in late 1978 the then Labour government had presided over a profound crisis inside. The government's abject failure to resolve it laid the foundations for the 25-day disturbance at Strangeways, the longest in prison history (Sim, 2009). However, for her, and other potential Labour ministers, the election of the Conservative/ Liberal coalition government in 2010 was year zero. There was no recognition of the penal policy failures (or any other policy failures for that matter) of previous Labour governments before that year. The depth of the crisis in 2023 and 2024 testified to the decades of failure of *successive* governments to move beyond the endless cycle of crisis/reform/crisis/reform.

And in another shameless intervention during the General Election campaign, Mahmood indicated that a future Labour government would make it easier to deliver the 20,000 new prison places promised by the Conservative government by allowing ministers, rather than local authorities, to decide where new prisons could be built thereby avoiding being 'bogged down by backbencher complaints and the planning process' (cited in Sparrow, 2024).

New government, old compromises

After the General Election, Mahmood was appointed as the new Secretary of State for Justice. When she spoke about the ongoing crisis, she blamed the previous government and maintained that Labour's early release scheme was 'now [the] one way to avert disaster' (Gov. UK, 2024a). And while 1000 new trainee probation officers were to be introduced by March 2025, the implications of this policy were lost in a blizzard of apocalyptic images:

> When no cells are available, suspects cannot be held in custody. *This means vanloads of dangerous people circling the country, with nowhere to go* [...] We could see looters running amok, smashing in windows, robbing shops and setting neighbourhoods alight. In short, if we fail to act now, we face the collapse of the criminal justice system. *And a total breakdown of law and order.* This is not the plot of some dystopian film. This crisis is now very close indeed (Gov.UK, 2024a, emphasis added).

At this profound moment, she had an opportunity to start a different but less electorally-attractive debate about prisons and discuss many of the issues highlighted by prisoners' rights organisations and charities including the routine failure of previous governments to implement recommendations made by the Prisons Inspectorate, the Prisons and Probation Ombudsman and coroners about prison policy in general, and preventable deaths, in particular. She ignored this indefensible failure. Instead, she focussed on what politicians always assume is a vote-winning policy, namely building more prisons more quickly through, as noted above, 'taking control of the planning process' while also designating them as institutions of 'national importance' (Gov.UK, 2024a). However, if the prison building programme was the answer then, like her predecessors, she was asking the wrong questions.

By August 2024, the crisis had intensified. Jailing hundreds of people for their involvement in the racist and Islamophobic riots in the summer further increased the prison population. And once again, Wandsworth was the subject of scathing criticisms from the prison's Independent Monitoring Board (IMB) who described conditions as 'inhumane' and 'dangerously overcrowded' (Independent Monitoring Boards, 2024c: 10). Furthermore:

> There were ten deaths in custody (DIC) (2022/23: four) during the reporting period, seven were foreign nationals (FNs). Six were apparently self-inflicted; three of these men were on an ACCT. Four apparently died from natural causes […] *The Board was concerned that on a number of occasions the prison failed to inform the IMB of the DIC in a timely manner* (Independent Monitoring Boards, 2024c: 15, emphasis added).

There were also systemic problems in the Assessment, Care in Custody and Teamwork (ACCT) system which was supposed to support those who were at risk of self-harm. Despite these incidents rising to 998, or nearly 3 a day, 'the timing and location of ACCT reviews was haphazard, making it difficult for other agencies to attend and healthcare attendance at ACCT reviews, was neither regular nor consistent' (Independent Monitoring Boards, 2024: 16).

Two members of staff, who were part of a 27 strong WhatsApp group, were sacked after joking about the death of a prisoner. Amongst other terms, the dead prisoner was described as a 'fuckwit', 'former fuckwit', 'total prick'. One said that he 'hope[d] he suffered' while others:

> […] joked about assaulting prisoners […] and talked about getting revenge on an inmate who assaulted a member of staff. Officers were

also said to have posted misogynistic messages, mocked a gay prison officer's appearance, joked that a gay prisoner particularly enjoyed jail shower time and referenced colleagues' drug use (Siddique, 2024).

The new government responded to the more general crisis in capacity by implementing its own early release scheme involving nearly 1800 prisoners. In response to an interview with a serving governor, Labour fell back on the old myths about people in prison, arguing that ministers were 'taking the difficult but necessary action to make sure *we can keep locking up dangerous criminals and keep people safe*' (Sky News, 2024, emphasis added).

Given the depth of the crisis, it might have been expected that the Justice Secretary would have used her speech at the Labour Party conference in September (2024) to discuss her intentions. Instead, she spoke for only 15 minutes and defended the early release scheme by, once again, blaming the previous government for the crisis. Beyond that, her speech was short on policy announcements, except for one. She argued, correctly, that as prison did not work for women, the number inside could be reduced through using more community sentences and diverting women from custody by resolving cases before they went to court. While this intervention was welcome, she missed a key point. Introducing non-custodial alternatives, while simultaneously regarding 'prison as the inevitable backup' to them meant they were 'not going to work' (Carlen, 1990: 121). Furthermore:

[...]we cannot expect any punishment to 'work' unless we have also addressed the other factors, which might be called, collectively, factors of 'social justice' – housing, income, health, education and employment. But structural factors alone are insufficient [...] women offenders need to feel that they are people of worth who can sustain and be sustained in reciprocal rather than subordinate or exploitative relationships (Carlen and Worrall, 2004: 152).

With the women's population projected to rise to 3900 by September 2028 (Ministry of Justice, 2024g: 15), then the Justice Secretary's plans are, indeed, 'not going to work' unless the issues discussed above are seriously addressed.

In October 2024, the crisis in capacity led to the early release of another 1100 prisoners. It also led to the Justice Secretary announcing a review of sentencing. Shockingly, the review was *not* asked to consider the scandal of IPP sentences, nor the remand system, both of which were driving the prison population upwards. And while emphasising that more alternatives to prison were needed, she maintained that the building programme would continue, thereby ignoring, not for the first time, one of the key lessons from prison history; more prisons mean more people inside. The possibility that the average daily population could rise to between 95,700 and 105,200 by March 2029 (Ministry of Justice, 2024g: 3) provided a grim warning for the future and underlined the fallacy of short-term expedient reforms.

The projected rise was not surprising given the Justice Secretary's emphasis on prisons and punishment. While she maintained that 'those prisoners who earned[ed] the right to turn their lives around should be encouraged to do so', she also made it clear that she 'believ[ed] in punishment. I believe in prison, but I also believe that we must increase the range of punishments we use'. The review would 'make sure prison and punishment work - and that there is always a cell waiting for dangerous offenders' (Gov.UK, 2024b). As for 'prolific offenders', the review would 'consider whether a longer sentence might punish them better and force them to engage with rehabilitation on the inside' (Hansard, 2024b: column. 198). However, she failed to mention the current lack of accredited rehabilitation programmes, nor the restricted access to those programmes which are available. Furthermore, as Chapter 4 illustrated, purposeful activity is limited to the point of being virtually non-existent.

Finally, she was said to be considering a scheme used in Texas prisons as a potential model for rehabilitation programmes in England and Wales (Syal, 2024b). Leaving aside the criticisms which have been made of the scheme (Deitch, 2024), if true, the idea of transplanting policy from a system which, historically, has been renowned for its brutality and racism was astonishing (Perkinson, 2010). The use of containment cages for people in solitary confinement which were smaller than a telephone booth and which had no toilet or sink (Busby, 2024) and the number of deaths in state custody – over 14,000 between 2005 and June 2024, disproportion- ately involving Hispanic and Black people with over 11,300 occurring in prisons and jails alone (Texas Justice Initiative, 2024) – should have been enough to give her serious pause for thought about implementing *any* policy from Texas prisons.

In April 2025, in a further illustration of the pernicious, authoritarian policies being pursued by the Labour government, Mahmood threat- ened to pass emergency legislation to over-rule new guidelines from the Sentencing Council whose goal was to promote more consistency in sen- tencing practices, ensure judicial independence and increase the public's understanding of sentencing. The guidelines would have:

[...] required magistrates and judges to consult a pre-sentence report before deciding whether to imprison someone of an ethnic or religious minority, alongside other groups including young adults, abuse survivors and mothers. It would have taken into account structural disparities in sentencing outcomes, such as the high risk of stillbirth that pregnant women face in prison and the damage caused by separating mothers from children. It would also have introduced measures to combat racism in courts (Starling, 2025).

However, following criticism from Robert Jenrick, the Shadow Justice Secretary, who argued without irony that the guidelines were 'biased against "straight white men" and amounted to "two-tier justice"' (Zeffman and Nevitt, 2025), the Justice Secretary 'chose to perform a populist pan- tomime'. Her claim that:

'[...] there will never be a two-tier sentencing approach under my watch' was foolish and dangerous. Instead of challenging the dog- whistle slogan, she legitimised it, which then triggered its repetition across the press. When the Sentencing Council stuck to its guns,

Mahmood threatened to pass emergency legislation to overrule it. The council, browbeaten, suspended the implementation of the guideline. It is infuriating to see another Labour government seek to appease a rightwing voter base by reinforcing the 'tough on crime' doom loop that has gridlocked our justice system for the past 30 years (Starling, 2025)

A world without prisons

This book began with considering the crisis in safety facing people in prison which was illustrated by the scandalous number of deaths and incidents of self-harm inside. It finishes with data which illustrates that this crisis remained ongoing at the end of 2024. In the 12 months to December, there were 342 deaths, up 10% from the previous 12 months. There were 89 self-inflicted deaths, down 7% in the same period. Ominously, in the last quarter of 2024, there were 110 deaths, an increase of 31% from the previous quarter. Self-inflicted deaths had risen by 53% to 29 in the same quarter. And in the 12 months to September 2024, there were 77,869 reported incidents of self-harm – a rate of 891 per 1000 prisoners – an increase of 15% from the previous 12 months. In women's prisons there were 5906 incidents per 1000 prisoners. This was more than eight times higher than in men's prisons notwithstanding a 14% increase in the number of male prisoners and a 2% decrease in the number of women prisoners (Ministry of Justice, 2025).

And yet, despite this data, and the grim reality of life inside they represent, prisons remain pivotal to the iron-clad, authoritarian mentality which has gripped the major political parties in their frantic, futile attempt to maintain the decaying social order of a fractured society dismembered by searing, structural, social inequality. In this desolate, historical moment, a remorseless and ruthless state machine continues to police, punish and traumatise those on the bottom rung of the ladder of inequality. At the same time, as this book has shown, policing the corrosive crimes and social harms of those at the top of this ladder, responding seriously to their culpability and holding then accountable for their actions and non-actions, remains fragmentary to the point of being virtually non-existent. In effect, it is a society where the 'rich get richer and the poor get prison' (Reiman and Leighton, 2012).

As the debate about law, order and prisons has become more toxic, more ill-informed and more politically expedient – often reinforced by the 'unprecedented levels of secrecy, obfuscation, dissembling and downright lying that now characterise public life' (Panitch and Leys: 2005: vii) – so the degradation and dehumanisation of those caught in the pliers of state power has become more intense. State agents, the media, despite some honourable exceptions, the Prison Officers Association, politicians and carefully chosen 'experts', share a regressive echo-chamber. These interconnected groups have emphasised different policy goals, at different historical moments. And while the emphasis might have changed over the centuries, the *outcomes* have been the same: pain, punishment and ignominy for the minority of law breakers relentlessly targeted and callously prodded and processed through the landings and wings of different state- and privately-run institutions.

In this context, it is important to remember that prisons are anything but 'natural'. They are a human construction. And like any human construction, they can be dismantled and replaced with a radically different system which *will* provide safety, security, protection and social justice for all, including people in prison. Breaking free from the debilitating and depressing cycle of crisis/reform/crisis/reform – in the words of Samuel Beckett, 'Try again. Fail again. Fail better' (Power, 2016) – and transcending 'acceptable', political and populist common sense about the institution, is a difficult, though not impossible task. Implementing the abolitionist programme outlined above would fundamentally transform this system, shifting it away from punishment and injustice to one based on compassion and social justice.

Rather than dismissing abolitionists as romantic idealists, their critics might consider the importance of utopian thinking which underpins abolitionism and remember that 'practical reforms depend on utopian dreaming – or at least utopian thinking drives incremental improvements' (Jacoby, cited in Sim, 2009: 162). And instead of their often-condescending dismissal of abolitionist policies, they might also think about engaging with these policies and recognise their capacity for delivering the transformational change that is desperately needed. Critics of abolitionism are not ignorant about the dire state of prisons, nor about the destructive impact they have on people inside, nor about the abject failure to fulfil their official goals. Acting on this knowledge, and engaging with abolitionist arguments, would mean that they could become part of the solution to the 200-year-old, systemic prison crisis, rather than continuing to be part of the problem through their misguided belief in instituting reforms to a system which, as the history in this book has shown, is incapable of being reformed.

Given this history, failing to turn the possibility of abolishing prisons into the probability that they *will* be abolished means continuing to support unforgiving, zombie institutions like Wandsworth, whose final burial is long overdue. Standing over its grave would be a redemptive system based on care, compassion, equality, democratic accountability and social justice for all, including for victims and survivors, which the current system is dismally failing to provide. This radically transformed criminal injustice system would operate within a radically transformed political economy devoid of the lacerating social divisions which diminish and destroy the potential for human and humane growth. To be replaced with what? For abolitionists, the answer is a society based on collective, social need rather than individual, anti-social greed.

Writing in 1983, Steven Box noted that: 'We have for too long ignored crimes of the powerful, allowed the poor to be imprisoned scapegoats, and encouraged criminal justice personnel to act subversively. Justice has suffered, and so have we all' (Box, 1983: 223).

Over 40 years on, who could disagree with Box's compelling point?

further reading

Carlen, P. (1990) *Alternatives to Women's Imprisonment* Milton Keynes: Open University Press. This classic book provides a compelling argument for abolishing women's prisons as well as outlining a range of policies which would radically transform the situation of women in prison and in the wider criminal injustice system.

Coyle, M. and Scott, D. (eds) (2021) *The Routledge International Handbook of Penal Abolition* London: Routledge. This edited collection discusses contemporary, abolitionist praxis and utilises prisoners' voices to support the argument for abolishing prisons.

Davis, A. (2003) *Are Prisons Obsolete?* New York: Seven Sisters Press. This book points to the historical gaps in abolitionist praxis concerning the racialisation of punishment, an issue which has intensified since the book was first published.

Law, V. (2021) *'Prisons Make Us Safer' and 20 other Myths About Mass Incarceration* Boston: Beacon Press. This is an excellent dissection of the myths surrounding prisons which justify their existence, particularly with respect to violence against women and girls.

Mathiesen, T. (2006) *Prison on Trial* Winchester: Waterside Press. This book outlines the case for prison abolition through a detailed critique of the traditional defences of the prison, such as deterrence, rehabilitation and incapacitation.

Scott, D. (2018) *Against Imprisonment: An Anthology of Abolitionist Essays* Hook: Waterside Press. This collection of essays discusses the development of abolitionist praxis and resistance and the need to replace punishment as a justification for prisons.

Scott, D. (2020) *For Abolition: Essays on Prisons and Socialist Ethics* Hook: Waterside Press. This collection of essays is built on prisoners' testimonies which serve as a starting point for exploring the interlocking relationship between morality, ethics, prisons and abolition.

Whynacht, A. (2021) *Insurgent Love: Abolition and Domestic Homicide* Halifax: Fernwood Publishing. Written from a feminist, abolitionist position, this book addresses one of the most profound questions facing abolitionists: what should be done with violent offenders?

Activist websites

The websites below represent groups who campaign for radical transformation in prisons and the wider criminal injustice system. They are also an excellent resource for data and reports. Becoming a member, and/or offering financial support to one or more of them will help to further the cause of social justice.

Abolitionist Futures (https://abolitionistfutures.com/)
Black Lives Matter UK (https://blacklivesmatter.uk/)
Centre for Crime and Justice Studies (https://www.crimeandjustice.org.uk/)
European Group for the Study of Deviance and Social Control
    (www.european-group.org/)
INQUEST (inquest.org.uk)
Joint Enterprise Not Guilty by Association (https://jengba.co.uk/)
Rape Crisis England and Wales (https://rapecrisis.org.uk/)
United Group for Reform of IPP (https://www.ungripp.com/)
Women in Prison (https://womeninprison.org.uk/)

Newspaper

Inside Time (https://insidetime.org/) provides a voice for people in prison, and their families.

references

Acheson, I. (2024) *Screwed* Hull: Biteback Publishing

Atkinson, K., Monk, H. and Sim, J. (2023) 'Traumatising the Traumatised: Self-Harm and Death in Women's Prisons in England and Wales' in Atkinson, K., Barr, U. Monk, H. and Tucker, K. (eds) *Feminist Responses to Injustices of the State and Its Institutions: Politics, Interventions, Resistance* Bristol: Bristol University Press pp 199–215

Baldwin, J. (1972) *No Name in the Street* New York: The Dial Press

Bawden, A. (2024) 'Prisoners with cancer in England more likely to die of it than other patients' *The Guardian*, 30 April www.theguardian.com/society/2024/apr/29/prisoners-with-cancer-england-more-likely-die Accessed 30 April 2024

BBC (2024) *The World This Weekend* Radio 4, 18 August

Behan, C. and Stark, A. (2023) *Prisons and Imprisonment: An Introduction* Cham: Palgrave Macmillan

Bell, M. (2021) 'Abolition: A New Paradigm for Reform' *Law and Policy Review*, Volume *46*, Issue 1, pp 32–68 DOI: https://doi.org/10.1017/lsi.2020.21 Accessed 23 October 2023

Bhui, H. S. (2024) *What Are Prisons For?* Bristol: Bristol University Press

Blakeley, G. (2024) *Vulture Capitalism: Corporate Crimes, Backdoor Bailouts and the Death of Freedom* London: Bloomsbury

Box, S. (1983) *Power, Crime and Mystification* London: Tavistock

Boyle, J. (1984) *The Pain of Confinement* Edinburgh: Canongate

Burnett, J. (2022) *Work and the Carceral State* London: Pluto

Busby, J. (2024) 'This might be the worst thing happening in Texas right now' *Slate*, 20 October https://slate.com/news-and-politics/2024/10/worst-thing-happening-texas-prison-conditions.html Accessed 23 October 2024

Butler, P. (2022) 'Over 330,000 excess deaths in Great Britain linked to austerity, finds study' *The Guardian*, 5 October www.theguardian.com/business/2022/oct/05/over-330000-excess-deaths-in-great-britain-linked-to-austerity-finds-study Accessed 22 June 2024

Carlen, P. (1988) *Women, Crime and Poverty* Milton Keynes: Open University Press

Carlen, P. (1990) *Alternatives to Women's Imprisonment* Milton Keynes: Open University Press

Carlen, P. (2012) *Against Rehabilitation for Reparative Justice* Twenty Second Lecture in Honour of Eve Saville London, 6 November

Carlen, P. and Worrall, A. (2004) *Analysing Women's Imprisonment* Cullompton: Willan

Carrier, N. and Piché, J. (2015) 'The State of Abolitionism', *Penal Field* Volume *12*, no page numbers https://doi.org/10.4000/champpenal.9164 Accessed 11 November 2023

Chambliss, W. and Mankoff, M. (eds) (1976) *Whose Law? What Order?* New York: Wiley

Coles, D. and Shaw, H. (no date) *Learning from Death in Custody Inquests: A New Framework for Action and Accountability* London: INQUEST

Council of Europe (2020) *Report to the United Kingdom Government on the visit to the United Kingdom carried out by the European Committee for the Prevention of Torture and Inhuman or Degrading Treatment or Punishment (CPT) from 13 to 23 May 2019* Strasbourg: Council of Europe

Crace, J. (2023) 'Digested week: Space for one more in Tories' brave new world – after a fuss' *The Guardian*, 20 October www.theguardian.com/uk-news/2023/oct/20/digested-week-space-for-one-more-in-tories-brave-new-world-after-a-fuss Accessed 16 November 2023

Cunliffe, J. and Morrison, G. (2023) 'Demystifying Injustice: Joint Enterprise Law and Miscarriages of Justice' in Scott, D. and Sim, J. (eds) *Demystifying Power, Crime and Social Harm: The Work and Legacy of Steven Box* London: Palgrave Macmillan pp 481–505

Davis, A. (no date) *History is a Weapon: Masked Racism: Reflections on the Prison Industrial Complex* www.historyisaweapon.com/defcon1/davisprison.html Accessed 28 June 2024

Davis, A. (2003) *Are Prisons Obsolete?* New York: Seven Sisters Press

Davies, E., Obolenskaya, P., Francis, B., Blom, N., Phoenix, J., Pullerits, M. and Walby, S. (2024) 'Definition and Measurement of Violence in the Crime Survey for England and Wales: Implications for the Amount and Gendering of Violence' *The British Journal of Criminology* https://academic.oup.com/bjc/advance-article/doi/10.1093/bjc/azae050/7724637 Accessed 30 August 2024

Deitch, M. (2024) 'The UK looks to Texas for prison solutions – but is it looking through rose-coloured glasses?', Centre for Crime and Justice Studies, www.crimeandjustice.org.uk/uk-looks-texas-prison-solutions-it-looking-through-rose-coloured-glasses Accessed 22 October 2024

Dodd, V. (2024) 'Police chiefs say prison crisis in England and Wales is "unsustainable"' *The Guardian*, 21 May www.theguardian.com/society/

article/2024/may/21/police-chiefs-say-prison-crisis-in-england-and-wales-is-unsustainable Accessed 25 May 2024

Dorling, D. (2024) *Shattered Nation: Inequality and the Geography of a Failing State* London: Verso

Dugan, E. (2024) '"Very dangerous and confusing": one inmate's view on joint enterprise law' *The Guardian*, 1 February www.theguardian.com/law/2024/feb/01/very-dangerous-and-confusing-one-inmates-view-on-joint-enterprise-law Accessed 17 April 2024

Elkins, C. (2022) *Legacy of Violence: A History of the British Empire* London: The Bodley Head

End Violence Against Women (2023) 'Latest data shows the criminal justice system isn't working for women', 21 July www.endviolenceagainstwomen.org.uk/latest-data-shows-the-criminal-justice-system-isnt-working-for-women/ Accessed 15 March 2024

Epstein, R. (2022) 'The rich go to rehab – the poor go to prison: imprisonment for contempt of court', Is It A Crime to be Poor Alliance?, 5 January https://crimetobepoor.org/2022/01/05/the-rich-go-to-rehab-%e2%88%92-the-poor-go-to-prison-imprisonment-for-contempt-of-court/ Accessed 13 July 2024

Evans, P. (1986) 'Big expenditure on new prisons a "costly failure"' *The Times*, 6 November: 5

Eves, K. (2023) *The Brook House Inquiry Report Volume I* London: HMSO HC 1789-I

Fisher, M. (2009) *Capitalist Realism: Is There No Alternative?* London: Zed Books

Fitzgerald, M. and Sim, J. (1982) *British Prisons* Oxford: Basil Blackwell 2nd edition

Foucault, M. (1979) *Discipline and Punish: The Birth of the Prison* Harmondsworth: Peregrine

Foucault, M. (2003) *Society Must Be Defended* London: Penguin

Fousiani, K. and van Prooijen, J-W. (2023) 'Motives for Punishing Powerful Vs. Powerless Offenders: The Mediating Role of Demonization' Victims and Offenders' *An International Journal of Evidence-based Research, Policy, and Practice*, Volume *18*, Issue 6 www.tandfonline.com/doi/full/10.1080/15564886.2022.2069899#abstract Accessed 11 September 2024

Garland, D. (1985) *Punishment and Welfare* Aldershot: Gower

Garland, D. (1990) *Punishment and Modern Society: A Study in Social Theory* Oxford: Clarendon

Gecsoyler, S. (2023) 'UN highlights "psychological harm" to UK man jailed since 2012 for phone theft' *The Guardian*, 3 September www.theguardian.com/law/2023/sep/03/un-highlights-psychological-harm-to-uk-man-jailed-since-2012-for-phone-theft Accessed 14 May 2024

Gilroy, P. (2013) *There Ain't No Black in the Union Jack* London: Routledge

Goodier, M. (2024) 'Schools, hospitals and prisons among England's crumbling public buildings' *The Guardian*, 27 December www.theguardian.com/society/2024/dec/27/schools-hospitals-prisons-england-public-buildings-disrepair Accessed 1 January 2025

Gov.UK (2024a) 'New Lord Chancellor sets out measures to avert prison capacity crisis' Gov.UK www.gov.uk/government/speeches/new-lord-chancellor-sets-out-measures-to-avert-prison-capacity-crisis Accessed 13 August 2024

Gov.UK (2024b) 'Landmark Sentencing Review launched to end prison crisis' *Press Release*, 21 October Accessed 22 October 2024

Grover, C. (2019) 'Violent proletarianisation: social murder, the reserve army of labour and social security "austerity" in Britain' *Critical Social Policy*, Volume *39*, Issue 3, https://journals.sagepub.com/doi/full/10.1177/0261018318816932 Accessed 20 November 2020

Hall, S., Massey, D. and Rustin, M. (2013) 'After neoliberalism: analysing the present' *Soundings*, Issue 53 pp 8–22

Halliday, J. (2024) '"DWP are the real criminals": carer in tatters after "brutal" fraud prosecution' *The Guardian*, 7 April www.theguardian.com/society/2024/apr/07/dwp-carer-allowance-benefit-payment-case Accessed 8 April

Halpert, M. (2024) 'Glynn Simmons: Freedom "exhilarating" for man exonerated after 48 years' *BBC News*, 6 January www.bbc.co.uk/news/world-us-canada-67878504 Accessed 7 January 2024

Hansard (1982) *House of Lords Official Report, 24 March, Law and Order* Columns 967–1053 London: Her Majesty's Stationary Office

Hansard (2023) *House of Commons* 15 November, Volume 740, Columns 639–648 London: Her Majesty's Stationary Office

Hansard (2024a) 'IPP Sentences' Volume *755*, 29 October London: House of Commons

Hansard (2024b) 'Sentencing Review and Prison Capacity' Volume 755, 22 October London: House of Commons

Hansard (2025) 'Offenders Suicide' *Daily Report*, 24 February https://qna.files.parliament.uk/qnadailyreports/Written-Questions-Answers-Statements-Daily-Report-Commons-2025-02-24.pdf Accessed 2 March 2025

Hattenstone, S. (2024) 'Tommy Nicol was kind and friendly – a beloved brother. Why did he die in prison on a '99-year' sentence?' *The Guardian*, 24 April www.theguardian.com/society/2024/apr/24/tommy-nicol-kind-friendly-beloved-brother-died-prison-99-year-sentence Accessed 24 April 2024

Health and Safety Executive (2024) 'RIDIND: Work-related injuries reported under RIDDOR by detailed industry', *Index of Data Tables* www.hse.gov.uk/statistics/tables/index.htm Accessed 26 November 2024

Herskind, M. (2021) *Presentation: Understanding the Abolition Movement* https://princetonlibrary.org/videos/presentation-understanding-the-abolition-movement/ Accessed 25 November 2024

HM Chief Inspector of Prisons for England and Wales (2023) *Annual Report 2022–23* London: HM Inspectorate of Prisons

HM Inspectorate of Prisons (2018a) *Report on an unannounced inspection of HMP and YOI Nottingham 11–12 December 2017 and 8–11 January 2018* London: Her Majesty's Inspectorate of Prisons

HM Inspectorate of Prisons (2018b) *Urgent notification: HM Prison Exeter* www.justiceinspectorates.gov.uk/hmiprisons/wp-content/uploads/sites/4/2018/05/Exeter-UN-letter-and-debrief-for-publication.pdf Accessed 10 June 2018

HM Inspectorate of Prisons (2019) *Report on an unannounced inspection of HMP Eastwood Park* London: Her Majesty's Inspectorate of Prisons

HM Inspectorate of Prisons (2020) *Report on an unannounced inspection of HMP Warren Hill by HM Chief Inspector of Prisons* London: HM Inspectorate of Prisons

HM Inspectorate of Prisons (2022a) *Thematic review. The experiences of adult black male prisoners and black prison staff by HM Chief Inspector of Prisons December 2022* London: HM Inspectorate of Prisons

HM Inspectorate of Prisons (2022b) *Report on an unannounced inspection of HMP Garth by HM Chief Inspector of Prisons 7–18 November 2022* London: HM Inspectorate of Prisons

HM Inspectorate of Prisons (2023a) *Preparing prisoners for release* London: HM Inspectorate of Prisons www.justiceinspectorates.gov.uk/hmiprisons/chief-inspectors-blog/preparing-prisoners-for-release/ Accessed 14 November 2023

HM Inspectorate of Prisons (2023b) *Report on an unannounced inspection of HMP Lowdham Grange by HM Chief Inspector of Prisons 15–26 May 2023* London: HM Inspectorate of Prisons

HM Inspectorate of Prisons (2023c) *Report on an unannounced inspection of HMP Dartmoor by HM Chief Inspector of Prisons 19 June–6 July 2023* London: HM Prisons Inspectorate

HM Inspectorate of Prisons (2024a) *Report on an unannounced inspection of HMP Bedford by HM Chief Inspector of Prisons 30 October–9 November 2023* London: HM Inspectorate of Prisons

HM Inspectorate of Prisons (2024b) *Urgent Notification: HMP Rochester* https://cloud-platforme218f50a4812967ba1215eaecede923f.s3.amazonaws.com/uploads/sites/19/2024/09/HMP-Rochester-Urgent-Notification-Letter-.pdf Accessed 31 October 2024

Hobbs, S. (2023) Letter *The Guardian*, 26 January www.theguardian.com/
uk-news/2023/jan/26/zara-aleena-was-failed-by-a-privatised-probation-
service Accessed 27 January 2023

House of Commons Health and Social Care Committee (2018) *Prison health
Twelfth Report of Session 2017–19 Report, together with formal minutes
relating to the report* London: House of Commons HC 963

House of Commons Justice Committee (2019) *Prison Governance First Report of
Session 2019* London: House of Commons HC191

Howard League for Penal Reform (2014) *Breaking point: Understaffing and
overcrowding in prisons Research briefing* https://howardleague.org/
wp-content/uploads/2016/03/Breaking-point-10.07.2014.pdf Accessed 23
August 2024

Howard League for Penal Reform (2020) *Reset: Rethinking remand for women*
London: Howard League for Penal Reform

Hudson, B. (1993) *Penal Policy and Social Justice* Basingstoke: Macmillan

Ignatieff, M. (1978) *A Just Measure of Pain* Basingstoke: MacMillan

Independent Monitoring Boards (2019) *IMB National Annual Report 2017/18*
London: National Preventive Mechanism

Independent Monitoring Boards (2022a) *National Annual Report 2021–22 October
2022* London: National Preventive Mechanism

Independent Monitoring Boards (2022b) *Annual Report of the Independent
Monitoring Board at HMP Wandsworth For reporting year 1 June 2021 to 31
May 2022* London: National Preventive Mechanism

Independent Monitoring Boards (2023) *Annual Report of the Independent
Monitoring Board at HMP Wandsworth For Reporting Year 1 June 2022 to 31
May 2023* London: National Preventative Mechanism

Independent Monitoring Boards (2024a) *Breaking point: the impact of a crumbling
prison estate on prisoners* https://imb.org.uk/news/breaking-point-the-impact-
of-a-crumbling-prison-estate-on-prisoners/ Accessed 28 November 2024

Independent Monitoring Boards (2024b) *Annual Report of the Independent
Monitoring Board at HMP Wormwood Scrubs For reporting year 1 June 2022
to 31 May 2023* London: National Preventive Mechanism

Independent Monitoring Boards (2024c) *Annual Report of the Independent
Monitoring Board at HMP Wandsworth* London: National Preventative
Mechanism

INQUEST (no date) *NO MORE DEATHS CAMPAIGN* London: INQUEST www.
inquest.org.uk/no-more-deaths-campaign Accessed 4 March 2024

INQUEST (2018) *Dying on the Inside: Examining Deaths in Women's Prisons*
London: INQUEST

INQUEST (2022a) 'INQUEST responds as new data shows 2021 had highest number of deaths in prison ever recorded' www.inquest.org.uk/moj-data-jan2022 Accessed 31 January 2022

INQUEST (2022b) *Deaths of racialised people in prison 2015–2022: Challenging racism and discrimination* London: INQUEST

INQUEST (2024a) 'Deaths of immigration detainees' www.inquest.org.uk/deaths-of-immigration-detainees Accessed 11 December 2024

INQUEST (2024b) 'Christine McDonald: jury finds neglect led to self-inflicted death at HMP Styal' *Media Release by Bhatt Murphy Reshared by INQUEST*, 10 May www.inquest.org.uk/christine-mcdonald-inquest-concludes Accessed 23 July 2024

INQUEST (2024c) 'Wayne Bayley: jury finds neglect contributed to the death of Black man from sickle cell disease complications and restraint at HMP Pentonville' *Media Release by Hickman and Rose Reshared by INQUEST*, 1 November www.inquest.org.uk/wayne-bayley-inquest Accessed 6 December 2024

Inside Time (2023) 'Tuck in! Food budget up 25%' *Inside Time*, 21 August https://insidetime.org/newsround/tuck-in-food-budget-up-25/ Accessed 8 July 2024

Jones, C. and Lally, C. (2024) *Prison population growth: drivers, implications and policy considerations* London: Parliamentary Office of Science and Technology, https://researchbriefings.files.parliament.uk/documents/POST-PB-0058/POST-PB-0058.pdf Accessed 30 January 2024

Jones, R., Hart, E. and and Scott, D. (2024) '"A pre-requisite of progress"? Prison modernisation and new prison building in England and Wales', *Criminology and Criminal Justice* https://doi.org/10.1177/14624745241229149 11 February 2024

Kersley, A. (2024) '"Worrying deterioration in safety" at UK immigration removal centres, warns chief inspector of prisons' *The Guardian*, 4 August www.theguardian.com/uk-news/article/2024/aug/04/worrying-deterioration-in-safety-at-uk-immigration-removal-centres-warns-chief-inspector-of-prisons Accessed 4 August 2024

Kotecha, S. (2024) 'Prison officers deal drugs and ask inmates for sex, BBC told' *BBC News*, 14 November www.bbc.com/news/articles/czd5r3m6rz6o Accessed 14 November 2024

Kotecha, S. (2025) 'Messages reveal prison staff violence towards inmates' *BBC News*, 2 April https://www.bbc.co.uk/news/articles/creqjllnr9no Accessed 2 April 2025

Lamble, S. (2022) 'Bridging the gap between reformists and abolitionists: can non-reformist reforms guide the work of prison inspectorates?',

Institute for Crime and Justice Policy Research, 22 March www.icpr.org.uk/news-events/2022/bridging-gap-between-reformists-and-abolitionists-can-non-reformist-reforms-guide Accessed 25 January 2025

Lammy Review (2017) *An independent review into the treatment of, and outcomes for, Black, Asian and Minority Ethnic individuals in the Criminal Justice System* https://assets.publishing.service.gov.uk/media/5a82009040f0b62305b91f49/lammy-review-final-report.pdf Accessed 2 April 2024

Law, V. (2021) *'Prisons Make Us Safer' And 20 other Myths About Mass Incarceration* Boston: Beacon Press

Lawrie, E. (2024) BBC News 'Victim-support cut to be devastating, charity says' *BBC News*, 4 December www.bbc.com/news/articles/cg4zqkpk962o Accessed 6 December 2024

Levine, J. and Meiners, E. J. (2020) *The Feminist and the Sex Offender* London: Verso

Liberty (2022) '5 THINGS YOU NEED TO KNOW ABOUT JOINT ENTERPRISE' www.libertyhumanrights.org.uk/issue/5-things-you-need-to-know-about-joint-enterprise/ Accessed 17 April 2024

Long, J. (2024) 'Parc Prison: three inmates hospitalised "in riot" over weekend – as one mother fears for son's life' *Channel 4 News* www.channel4.com/news/parc-prison-three-inmates-hospitalised-in-riot-over-weekend-as-one-mother-fears-for-sons-life Accessed 8 September 2024

Lynskey, D. (2024) *Everything Must Go: The Stories We Tell About the End of the World* London: Picador

Mathiesen, T. (1974) *The Politics of Abolition* London: Martin Robertson

Mathiesen, T. (1980) *Law, Society and Political Action* London: Academic Press

Mathiesen, T. (2000) *Prison on Trial* Winchester: Waterside Press 2nd edition

McClenaghan, M. (2023) 'More than 28,000 convicted of Covid rule breaches in England and Wales' *The Guardian*, 18 July www.theguardian.com/world/2023/jul/18/more-than-28000-convicted-of-covid-rule-breaches-in-england-and-wales Accessed 5 July 2024

McNeill, T. (2023) 'Prisoner suicides: why is the prison service immune from failure?', BCL Solicitors LLP www.bcl.com/news/prisoner-suicides-why-is-the-prison-service-immune-from-failure Accessed 17 January 2025

Meadows, C. (2023) 'Court reporter praised for shining light on use of Single Justice Procedure', Society of Editors, 16 August, www.societyofeditors.org/soe_news/court-reporter-praised-for-shining-light-on-use-of-single-justice-procedure/ Accessed 4 August 2024

Ministry of Justice (no date) *Deaths in Prison Custody 1978–2019* London: Ministry of Justice

Ministry of Justice (2023a) *Safety in Custody Statistics, England and Wales: Deaths in Prison Custody to September 2023 Assaults and Self-harm to June 2023* www.gov.uk/government/statistics/safety-in-custody-quarterly-update-to-june-2023/safety-in-custody-statistics-england-and-wales-deaths-in-prison-custody-to-september-2023-assaults-and-self-harm-to-june-2023 Accessed 26 October 2023

Ministry of Justice (2023b) *Deaths of offenders in the community, annual update to March 2023* London: Ministry of Justice www.gov.uk/government/statistics/deaths-of-offenders-in-the-community-annual-update-to-march-2023/deaths-of-offenders-in-the-community-annual-update-to-march-2023 Accessed 26 October 2023

Ministry of Justice (2024a) *Criminal Justice Statistics quarterly: June 2023* London: Ministry of Justice www.gov.uk/government/statistics/criminal-justice-system-statistics-quarterly-june-2023/criminal-justice-statistics-quarterly-june-2023-html Accessed 20 March 2024

Ministry of Justice (2024b) *Justice in Numbers pocketbook March 2024* London: Ministry of Justice

Ministry of Justice (2024c) *Offender management statistics quarterly: April to June 2024* www.gov.uk/government/statistics/offender-management-statistics-quarterly-april-to-june-2024/offender-management-statistics-quarterly-april-to-june-2024#licence-recalls Accessed 8 January 2025

Ministry of Justice (2024d) *Number of fixed-term and standard recalls of determinate-sentence offenders, January 2017 to September 2023* London: Ministry of Justice www.gov.uk/government/statistics/number-of-fixed-term-and-standard-recalls-of-determinate-sentence-offenders-january-2017-to-september-2023 Accessed 29 March 2024

Ministry of Justice (2024e) *Safety in Custody Statistics, England and Wales: Deaths in Prison Custody to December 2023 Assaults and Self-harm to September 2023* www.gov.uk/government/statistics/safety-in-custody-quarterly-update-to-september-2023/safety-in-custody-statistics-england-and-wales-deaths-in-prison-custody-to-december-2023-assaults-and-self-harm-to-september-2023 Accessed 25 January 2024

Ministry of Justice (2024f) *Costs per place and costs per prisoner by individual prison*. HM Prison & Probation Service Annual Report and Accounts 2022–23 Management Information Addendum Ministry of Justice Information Release, 21 March https://assets.publishing.service.gov.uk/media/65f4229810cd8e001136c655/costs-per-place-per-prisoner-2022-2023-summary.pdf Accessed 23 March 2024

Ministry of Justice (2024g) *Prison Population Projections 2024 to 2029, England and Wales* London: Ministry of Justice

Ministry of Justice (2024h) *HMPPS Annual Digest 2023 to 2024* London: Ministry of Justice www.gov.uk/government/statistics/hmpps-annual-digest-april-2023-to-march-2024/hmpps-annual-digest-2023-to-2024 Accessed 26 July 2024

Ministry of Justice (2025) *Safety in Custody Statistics, England and Wales: Deaths in Prison Custody to December 2024 Assaults and Self-harm to September 2024* www.gov.uk/government/statistics/safety-in-custody-quarterly-update-to-september-2024/safety-in-custody-statistics-england-and-wales-deaths-in-prison-custody-to-december-2024-assaults-and-self-harm-to-september-2024 Accessed 30 January 2025

Morran, D. (2022) 'Rejecting and retaining aspects of selfhood: constructing desistance from abuse as a "masculine" endeavour' *Criminology and Criminal Justice*, Volume 23, Issue 5 https://journals.sagepub.com/doi/full/10.1177/17488958211070365 Accessed 30 December 2024

Mott, J. (1985) *Adult Prisons and Prisoners in England and Wales 1970–1982 – A Review of the Findings of Social Research* London: HMSO

Murji, K. (2023) 'Institutional failure: policing in permacrisis' *Soundings*, Issue 83, pp 21–33

Nairn, T. (1988) *The Enchanted Glass: Britain and Its Monarchy* London: Radius

National Association of Probation Officers (1983) *Remands in Custody Briefing Paper* London: National Association of Probation Officers

National Audit Office (2024a) *An Overview of the Ministry of Justice for the New Parliament 2023–24* London: National Audit Office

National Audit Office (2024b) 'Prison expansion plan was "unrealistic and not prioritised" – NAO' *Press Release*, 4 December www.nao.org.uk/press-releases/prison-expansion-plan-was-unrealistic-and-not-prioritised-nao/ Accessed 4 December 2024

Office for National Statistics (2024a) *Homicide in England and Wales: year ending March 2023* Newport: Office for National Statistics https://cy.ons.gov.uk/peoplepopulationandcommunity/crimeandjustice/articles/homicideinenglandandwales/yearendingmarch2023 Accessed 1 July 2024

Office for National Statistics (2024b) *Domestic abuse in England and Wales overview: November 2024* www.ons.gov.uk/peoplepopulationandcommunity/crimeandjustice/bulletins/domesticabuseinenglandandwalesoverview/november2024 Accessed 28 November 2024

O'Neill, S. and Hayton, L (2025) 'Failure to act on coroner's advice blamed for thousands of deaths' *The Times*, 14 January www.thetimes.com/uk/

healthcare/article/failure-to-act-on-coroners-advice-blamed-for-thousands-of-deaths-8hlxqcp8q Accessed 19 January 2025

Osuh, C. (2024) 'Funding gap for women's centres will mean more prison sentences, experts warn' *The Guardian*, 22 December www.theguardian.com/society/2024/dec/22/womens-centres-england-and-wales-funding-gap-more-prison-sentences-experts-warn Accessed 22 December 2024

PA Media (2024) 'Man dies in detention at immigration removal centre near Gatwick airport' *The Guardian*, 29 October www.theguardian.com/uk-news/2024/oct/28/man-dies-in-detention-at-immigration-removal-centre-near-gatwick-airport Accessed 29 October 2024

Panitch, L. and Albo, G. (2017) 'Preface' in Panitch, L. and Albo, G. (eds) *The Socialist Register 2018* London: The Merlin Press pp ix–xiv

Panitch, L. and Leys, C. (2005) 'Preface' in Panitch, L. and Leys, C. (eds) *The Socialist Register 2006* London: The Merlin Press pp vii–x

Patel, A. (2024) '"Ground-breaking" prisoner apprenticeship scheme flops' FE Week, 26 January https://feweek.co.uk/ground-breaking-prisoner-apprenticeship-scheme-flops/ Accessed 10 February 2024

Perkinson, R. (2010) *Texas Tough: The Rise of America's Prison Empire* Toronto: Picador

Phillips, A. (2021) *On Getting Better* London: Picador

Pidd, H. (2024) 'Carer convicted over benefit error worth 30p a week fights to clear his name' *The Guardian*, 12 April www.theguardian.com/society/2024/apr/12/carers-allowance-benefit-error-30p-a-week-dwp Accessed 13 April 2024

Power, C. (2016) 'Samuel Beckett, the maestro of failure' *The Guardian*, 7 July www.theguardian.com/books/booksblog/2016/jul/07/samuel-beckett-the-maestro-of-failure Accessed 21 August 2024

Prisons and Probation Ombudsman (2022) *Annual Report 2021/22* London: Prisons and Probation Ombudsman CP738

Prisons and Probation Ombudsman (2024) *Learning Lessons Bulletin. Fatal Incident Investigations 19 Post-release death investigations 2* London: Prisons and Probation Ombudsman

Prison Reform Trust (1991) *The Identikit Prisoner: Characteristics of the Prison Population* London: Prison Reform Trust

Prison Reform Trust (2023a) 'Six in 10 women sent to prison serve sentences of less than six months' Prison Reform Trust, 16 October https://prisonreformtrust.org.uk/six-in-10-women-sent-to-prison-serve-sentences-of-less-than-six-months/?dm_i=47L,8GRNE,UF1XZ,YYYK3,1 Accessed 17 November 2023

Prison Reform Trust (2023b) *Prison: the facts. Bromley Briefings Summer 2023* London: Prison Reform Trust

Prison Reform Trust (2023c) *Bromley Briefings Prison Factfile January 2023* London: Prison Reform Trust

Prison Reform Trust (2024) *Bromley Briefings Prison Factfile February 2024* London: Prison Reform Trust

Private Eye (2023) No 1601, 30 June–13 July: 8

Private Eye (2024a) No 1620, 29 March –11 April: 38

Private Eye (2024b) No 1625, 7–20 June *2024*: 14

Raekstad, P. (2017) 'From Democracy to Socialism: Then and Now' in Panitch, L. and Albo, G. (eds) *The Socialist Register 2018* London: The Merlin Press pp 263–274

Ransby, B. (2015) 'The Class Politics of Black Lives Matter' Dissent, Fall www.dissentmagazine.org/article/class-politics-black-lives-matter/ Accessed 19 November 2024

Rape Crisis England and Wales (no date) 'Rape and Sexual Assault Statistics' https://rapecrisis.org.uk/get-informed/statistics-sexual-violence/ Accessed 21 February 2024

Rape Crisis England and Wales (2024) 'Rape Crisis centres at risk of closure without a commitment to continued funding after March 2025' https://rapecrisis.org.uk/news/rape-crisis-centres-at-risk-of-closure-without-a-commitment-to-continued-funding-after-march-2025/ Accessed 29 August 2024

Reed, A. (2022) 'Complaints handling in prisons' *The Investigator*, Issue 10 London: Prisons and Probation Ombudsman pp 3–6

Reiman, J. and Leighton, P. (2012) *The Rich Get Richer and the Poor Get Prison: Ideology, Class, and Criminal Justice* London: Routledge

Richards, G. and Davies, N. (2023) 'Performance Tracker 2023: Prisons Institute for Government', 30 October www.instituteforgovernment.org.uk/publication/performance-tracker-2023/prisons Accessed 26 August 2024

Rogerson, P. (2024) 'Budget '24: Justice spending to rise by £1.9bn' *The Law Society Gazette*, 30 October www.lawgazette.co.uk/news/budget-24-justice-spending-to-rise-by-19bn/5121376.article Accessed 30 October 2024

Ryan, M. and Sim, J. (1984) 'Decoding Leon Brittan' *The Abolitionist*, Volume 16 pp 3–7

Ryan, M. and Ward, T. (1989) *Privatisation and the Penal System* Stony Stratford: Open University Press

Sakande, N. (2021) 'Why are women being disproportionately penalised for TV licence non-payment?' Open Democracy www.opendemocracy.net/en/5050/why-are-women-being-disproportionately-penalised-tv-license-non-payment/ Accessed 20 January 2022

Sawyer, W. and Wagner, P. (2020) 'Mass Incarceration: The Whole Pie 2020' www.prisonpolicy.org/reports/pie2020.html Accessed 8 June 2021

Scott, D. (2008) 'Creating ghosts in the penal machine: prison officer occupational morality and the techniques of denial' in Bennett, J., Crewe, B. and Wahidin, A. (eds) *Understanding Prison Staff* Cullompton: Willan pp 168–186

Scott, D. (2018) *Against Imprisonment: An Anthology of Abolitionist Essays* Hook: Waterside Press

Scott, D. (2020a) *For Abolition: Essays on Prisons and Socialist Ethics* Hook: Waterside Press

Scott, D. (2020b) 'Prison officer violence: The crisis of visibility', *Centre for Crime and Justice Studies* www.crimeandjustice.org.uk/resources/prison-officer-violence-crisis-visibility Accessed 26 July 2024

Scott, D. and Sim, J. (2023) 'Steven Box: A '"Realist of a Larger Reality"' in Scott, D. and Sim, J. (eds) *Demystifying Power, Crime and Social Harm: The Work and Legacy of Steven Box* London: PalgraveMacmillan pp 3–53

Shaw, D. (2019) 'MoJ used failed sex offender treatment "unlawfully"' *BBC News*, 16 July www.bbc.com/news/uk-48998136 Accessed 4 July 2024

Showalter, E. (1987) *The Female Malady: Women, Madness and English Culture 1830–1980* London: Virago

Siddique, R. (2024) 'Jail staff sacked over messages mocking suicide of prisoner' *The Guardian*, 26 October www.theguardian.com/society/2024/oct/25/prison-officers-dismissed-for-joking-about-inmates-suicide Accessed 28 October 2024

Siddons, E. (2024) 'HMRC has not charged a single company over tax evasion under landmark legislation', *The Guardian*, 20 January www.theguardian.com/politics/2024/jan/20/hmrc-has-not-charged-a-single-company-over-tax-evasion-under-landmark-legislation Accessed 21 January 2024

Sim, J. (1990) *Medical Power in Prisons* Milton Keynes: Open University Press

Sim, J. (2004) 'The Victimised State and the Mystification of Social Harm' in Hillyard, P., Pantazis, C., Tombs, S. and Gordon, D. (eds) *Beyond Criminology: Taking Harm Seriously* London: Pluto pp 113–132

Sim, J. (2008) '"An inconvenient criminological truth": pain, punishment and prison officers' in Bennett, J., Crewe, B. and Wahidin, A. (eds) *Understanding Prison Staff* Cullompton: Willan pp 187–209

Sim, J. (2009) *Punishment and Prisons* London: Sage

Sim, J. (2018a) 'Beyond Redemption: The Barbarism of Birmingham Prison' Centre for the Study of Crime, Criminalisation and Social Exclusion https://ccseljmu.wordpress.com/2018/09/18/beyond-redemption-the-barbarism-of-birmingham-prison/ Accessed 21 March 2025

Sim, J. (2018b) 'Liverpool: A Broken Prison in a Broken System' Centre for the Study of Crime, Criminalisation and Social Exclusion https://ccseljmu.

wordpress.com/2018/01/30/liverpool-a-broken-prison-in-a-broken-system/ comment-page-1/ Accessed 21 March 2025

Sim, J. (2018c) 'Nottingham and Exeter Prisons: Death, Danger and Dehumanisation' Centre for the Study of Crime, Criminalisation and Social Exclusion https://ccseljmu.wordpress.com/2018/06/25/nottingham-and-exeter-prisons-death-danger-and-dehumanisation/ Accessed 21 March 2025

Sim, J. (2019) 'Shredding Human Beings: Death and Self-Harm in Prisons' *Centre for the Study of Crime, Criminalisation and Social Exclusion* https://ccseljmu. wordpress.com/2019/02/15/shredding-human-beings-death-and-self-harm-in-prisons/ Accessed 21 March 2025

Sim, J. (2023a) 'Confronting state power: dissenting voices and the demand for penal abolition' in Liebling, A., Maruna, S. and McAra, L. (eds) *The Oxford Handbook of Criminology* Oxford: Oxford University Press pp 884–908

Sim, J. (2023b) 'Punishment in "This Hard Land": Conceptualising the Prison in Power, Crime and Mystification' in Scott, D. and Sim, J. (eds) *Demystifying Power, Crime and Social Harm: The Work and Legacy of Steven Box* London: Palgrave Macmillan pp 507–530

Skeleton Argument of the Secretary of State (2020) in the High Court of Justice Queen's Bench Division Administrative Court Between: The Queen on the Application of Roy Davis Claimant-and-The Secretary of State for Justice C0/1389/2020

Sky News (2024) Broadcast, 19 September

Smith, S. (2024) 'More than a third of assaults on UK prison officers are not fully investigated' *The Observer*, 16 November www.theguardian.com/society/2024/nov/16/assaults-uk-prison-officers-not-investigated-abuse-inmates Accessed 17 November 2024

Sparrow, A. (2024) '"No tax surprises" in manifesto, Keir Starmer says – as it happened', *The Guardian*, 9 June www.theguardian.com/politics/live/2024/jun/09/uk-general-election-2024-live-rishi-sunak-keir-starmer-politics-latest-updates?filterKeyEvents=false&page=with:block-66657d2f8f083af419fdecc3 Accessed 9 June 2024

Starling, J. (2025) 'Labour's populist pantomime over sentencing rules plays into the hands of the right' *The Guardian*, 1 April https://www.theguardian.com/commentisfree/2025/apr/01/labour-prison-reform-justice-system Accessed 2 April 2025

Stewart, R. (2023) *Politics on the Edge: A Memoir from Within* London: Jonathan Cape

Sturge, G. (2024) *UK Prison Population Statistics* London: House of Commons Library

Sturge, G., McNair, L. and Carthew, H. (2023) *Estimates day: the spending of Ministry of Justice on His Majesty's Prisons and Probation Service* London: House of Commons Library

Syal, R. (2024a) 'Prison rehabilitation numbers in England and Wales down 74% since 2010, MoJ data shows' *The Guardian*, 1 July www.theguardian.com/society/article/2024/jul/01/prison-rehabilitation-numbers-down-74-since-2010-moj-data-shows Accessed 1 July 2024

Syal, R. (2024b) 'Judges could impose house arrest on criminals as part of major overhaul of sentencing' *The Guardian*, 21 October https://www.theguardian.com/law/2024/oct/21/england-and-wales-sentencing-overhaul-could-bring-in-home-detention Accessed 22 October 2024

Taylor, C. (2023) 'Urgent Notification: HMP Bedford' London: HM Inspectorate of Prisons https://committees.parliament.uk/publications/42215/documents/209771/default/ Accessed 20 November 2023

Taylor, D. (2019) 'Former prisoner sues Ministry of Justice over PTSD from rats' *The Guardian*, 29 January www.theguardian.com/society/2019/jan/29/former-prisoner-sues-ministry-of-justice-over-ptsd-from-rats Accessed 1 February 2019

Taylor, D. (2023a) 'Self-harm incident nearly every day in UK immigration detention, data shows' *The Guardian*, 27 November www.theguardian.com/uk-news/2023/nov/27/self-harm-incident-nearly-every-day-in-uk-immigration-detention-data-shows Accessed 27 November 2023

Taylor, D. (2023b) 'Germany refuses to extradite man to UK over concerns about British jail conditions' *The Guardian*, 5 September www.theguardian.com/society/2023/sep/05/germany-refuses-extradite-albanian-man-uk-jail-conditions Accessed 4 July 2024

Taylor, D. (2024) 'UK prison where baby died gives women rape alarms to call for help during labour', *The Guardian*, 21 January https://www.theguardian.com/society/2024/jan/21/uk-prison-hmp-bronzefield-pregnant-women-aisha-cleary Accessed 22 January 2024

Texas Justice Initiative (2024) 'Deaths in Custody' https://texasjusticeinitiative.org/datasets/custodial-deaths Accessed 23 October 2024

Tombs, S. (2016a) *Social Protection after the Crisis* Bristol: Policy Press

Tombs, S. (2016b) 'Prison deaths: a case of corporate manslaughter' *The Independent*, 2 December www.independent.co.uk/life-style/health-and-families/prison-deaths-a-case-of-corporate-manslaughter-a7451601.html Accessed 27 January 2025

Tombs, S. (2019) 'The Poor Get Prison... Grenfell as a Site of Crime?' Centre for the Study of Crime, Criminalisation and Social Exclusion https://ccseljmu.

wordpress.com/2019/12/06/the-poor-get-prison-grenfell-as-a-site-of-crime/ Accessed 1 December 2024

Tombs, S. (forthcoming) 'Justice After Grenfell? Crime, harm and structural inequality' *British Journal of Criminology*

Topping, A. (2025) '"Epidemic" of violence against women and girls in UK is getting worse – report' *The Guardian*, 31 January www.theguardian.com/society/2025/jan/31/violence-against-women-girls-epidemic-uk Accessed 31 January 2025

Toynbee, P. and Walker, D. (2017) *Dismembered: How the Conservative Attack on the State Harms Us All* London: Faber

UK Parliament Committees (2024) 'Parc deaths: some progress but much more to be done, Committee chair says' 11 December https://committees.parliament.uk/committee/162/welsh-affairs-committee/news/204344/parc-deaths-some-progress-but-much-more-to-be-done-committee-chair-says/ Accessed 29 January 2025

UK Parliament (2023) 'Prison Capacity' in Hansard, Volume *738*, column 59, 16 October London: UK Parliament https://hansard.parliament.uk/commons/2023-10-16/debates/50D29A75-C1E4-4FFC-A77D-11BBC20BCD99/PrisonCapacity Accessed 16 November 2023

United Group for Reform of IPP (no date) *What is the IPP Sentence?* https://www.ungripp.com/what-is-ipp Accessed 27 March 2025

Ussher, J. (1991) *Women's Madness: Misogyny or Mental Illness?* London: Harvester Wheatsheaf

Walker, P. (2024) 'Nearly 2,500 arrests in England and Wales since 2019 under Vagrancy Act', *The Guardian*, 7 April www.theguardian.com/society/2024/apr/07/homeless-people-arrested-vagrancy-act-england-wales-police Accessed 8 April 2024

Welsh, T. and Puri, N. (2025) 'Temporary housing linked to deaths of at least 74 children' *BBC News*, 28 January www.bbc.com/news/articles/c897d0l97jko Accessed 28 January 2025

Western, B. (2018) 'Violence, Poverty, Values, and the Will to Punish' in Kutz, C. (ed) *Didier Fassin: The Will to Punish* New York: Oxford University Press pp 129–141

Whynacht, A. (2021) *Insurgent Love: Abolition and Domestic Homicide* Halifax: Fernwood Publishing

Williams, M. (2023) 'Parliament's £180m expenses bonanza: photoshoots and business class flights' Open Democracy, 28 February www.opendemocracy.net/en/dark-money-investigations/parliament-expenses-scandal-mps-lords-claim-180m-flights-hotels-and-photoshoots/ Accessed 31 December 2024

Williams, Z. (2013) 'Why does Wonga even exist? It's a question no one on the left asks' *The Guardian*, 17 December www.theguardian.com/ commentisfree/2013/dec/17/why-wonga-exist-no-one-on-left-asks Accessed 19 November 2018

Williams, Z. (2024) 'The TV licence fee scandal: why are 1,000 people a week being casually criminalised?' *The Guardian*, 29 February www.theguardian.com/media/2024/feb/29/tv-licence-fee-scandal-1000-people-week-casually-criminalised Accessed 29 February 2024

Woodall, D. (2018) 'We Are All Criminals: The Abolitionist Potential of Remembering', *Social Justice*, Volume 45, No 4, pp 117–140

Wypijewski, J. (2024) 'Rule of Law?' Sidecar, 7 June https://newleftreview.org/sidecar/posts/rule-of-law?pc—1608 Accessed 9 June 2024

Zeffman, H. and Nevett, J. (2025) 'Sentencing guidelines ditched after two-tier row' *BBC News*, 31 March https://www.bbc.co.uk/news/articles/c5yg887m6qdo Accessed 4 April 2025

index